WOODROW WILSON *and the*
REBIRTH OF POLAND
1914–1920

WOODROW WILSON *and the*

REBIRTH OF POLAND

1914-1920

A Study in the Influence on American Policy

of Minority Groups of Foreign Origin

BY LOUIS L. GERSON

ARCHON BOOKS

1972

Library of Congress Cataloging in Publication Data

Gerson, Louis L
   Woodrow Wilson and the rebirth of Poland, 1914-
1920.

     Bibliography: p. 140-145
     1. Wilson, Woodrow, Pres. U. S., 1856-1924.
2. European War, 1914-1918—Territorial questions
—Poland.   3.   Poles in the United States. 4. U. S.
—Foreign relations—Poland.   5.   Poland—Foreign
relations—U. S. I. Title.
[D651.P7G4 1972]   327.73'0438   74-179575
ISBN 0-208-01229-X

*To Elizabeth and Elliot
and to my mother*

Preface

ONE OF THE HANDICAPS in making and administering American
foreign policy has been the susceptibility of minority groups
among our citizenry to propaganda and purposes of the land of
their origin, often contradicting the national interest of the United
States. This book is concerned with a striking instance of such
weakness. To be sure Poland regained her independence partly as a
result of fortuitous factors not of her own making like the first
World War, the Russian Revolution, and the victory of the Allied
Powers. But equally important was the personal influence of Woodrow Wilson. My purpose is to show how the patriotic leaders of the
movement for a new Polish nation worked on President Wilson
through the Polish immigrant population of the ·United States,
and the Polish-American vote, to secure the rebirth of Poland.

In this book I have examined the major political, social, religious, and ideological factors which brought about the rebirth of
Poland in the 20th century, an event which had seemed impossible
even to the most fanatically optimistic Polish patriots. Questions
of particular interest to me were: What were the opportunities during various phases of the first World War for a revival of Polish
sovereignty? What were the methods which the Polish-American
minority group used in influencing American foreign policy? How
much did Woodrow Wilson's influence contribute to the re-
establishment of Poland? It is my hope that this study of Wilson
and the rebirth of Poland may aid in understanding the Polish
problem of today as well as the broader problem of minority
groups and their effect on American foreign policy.

American historians have not studied this subject in any significant way. Some Polish as well as non-Polish historians, aware of the
importance of the first World War in the rebirth of Poland but desiring to give credit to the Polish people, have declared that the
Socialist movement in partitioned Poland played a vital role in the
re-creation of that state. I investigated this assertion not only to
clarify the Socialist role but also to get light on the Polish question,
on the Polish patriots, and on the Marxian and Bolshevik leaders
who ostensibly championed the Polish cause. There is sufficient evidence, hitherto unexplored, to suggest that in any event neither
Marxian, Bolshevik, Luxemburgian, nor Pilsudskian policy, nor

that of the Polish Socialists, could have achieved the unification of historically partitioned Polish territory or the independence of the country. My inquiries into the extent and character of Polish nationalism suggest also that its political significance has been overrated.

How then could Poland be reborn and become free and independent? Only a historical miracle could resurrect her: a European war in which one of the three partitioning powers must be arrayed against the other two, and in which all three would go down in defeat. In 1914 a European war did break out. But even such a war did not promise Polish independence. A thorough analysis of the policies of the Central and Allied Powers toward Poland reveals that no matter what combination of powers resulted from the war, a united, independent, and free Polish nation and state could not have been resurrected without the intervention of the United States and President Wilson and the diplomacy used at the Peace Settlement.

It has therefore been my primary aim to trace all the factors that influenced America's friendship toward Poland, which in turn determined the character of America's part in the restoration of Poland. To accomplish this I have devoted a considerable part of this book to a study of the Poles in America on the eve of the war; the attempts of Polish foreign leaders such as Paderewski and Dmowski to isolate them from American life; subsequent political pressure on the United States Government for early recognition of a Polish state; and finally Wilson's attitude toward the Polish Americans and the re-establishment of Poland.

With gratitude I acknowledge my debt to Professor Samuel Flagg Bemis. At every point in the planning of the original study, which was prepared as a doctoral dissertation at Yale University, and in the subsequent revisions for publication, I had the benefit and advantage of his wise and patient counsel. Without his encouragement and careful criticism this book could not have been written.

I wish also to express my appreciation to President Emeritus Charles Seymour who read the whole manuscript critically and gave me permission to quote from the private papers of Edward M. House.

Others who read the book and gave me the benefit of their suggestions are Professors Arnold Wolfers and Walter R. Sharp of

Yale University, and Dean George E. McReynolds and Professor Harry J. Marks of the University of Connecticut. The errors that remain are my own.

My sincere thanks go to Eugene Davidson, editor of the Yale University Press, and to Professor Lewis P. Curtis for their interest and valuable editorial suggestions. It was a pleasure to have the benefit of Miss Roberta Yerkes' help in editing the manuscript.

Louis L. Gerson

Contents

Illustrations

1. Introduction

IT WAS with a few perfunctory tears that the materialistic 18th century greeted the fall of Poland. On the eve of the fateful third partition of 1795 Poland was no longer a real nation. She was an unstable compound of two classes, the lower of which was entirely devoid of national sentiment, while the upper was divided into hostile religious sects and factions that could not unite even in extreme danger. To the upper class, the landed aristocracy, liberty meant the privilege of oppressing the lower class. Rousseau was right when he wrote that the "Polish Republic was composed of three orders; the nobles who are everything; the bourgeois who are nothing; and the peasants who are less than nothing." [1] How could the lower class, the abused peasantry, care for a country which had held them all in serfdom? Few were surprised when the Polish state, which existed only in name, came to an end.

The partitions of Poland did not shock 18th-century Europe. Even England did not resent them. What England did not like was the way the thing was done without her concurrence. Edmund Burke wrote:

> I have no doubt that a prince (Frederick the Great) so wise and politic will improve his new acquisitions (for I am not to call them conquests) to the best advantage for his power and greatness. I agree . . . that it was extremely fortunate that the three allied powers were able to find a fourth which was utterly unable to resist any of them, and much less all united. If this circumstance had not concurred with their earnest inclination to preserve public tranquility, they might have been obliged to find a discharge for the superfluous strength of their plethoric habits in the destruction of most of the countries in Europe. [2]

"Walpole," commented a contemporary writer, "is obviously more angry with the partitioning powers than sympathetic to the Poles, and what really annoys him is not the partition, but the re-

1. C. E. Vaughan, ed., *The Political Writings of Jean Jacques Rousseau* (Cambridge, Eng., Cambridge University Press, 1915), *2*, 442–3.
2. D. B. Horn, *British Public Opinion and the First Partition of Poland* (Edinburgh, Oliver and Boyd, 1915), pp. 13 and 14.

1

sulting interference with British trade in Dantzig." [3] Walpole himself wrote: ". . . whichever gets the better, the people will still remain slaves; I am pretty indifferent to which side (King or noble) the power of tyranny falls." [4]

The European continent greeted news of the partition as did England. "The Partition of Poland was committed under the eyes of an indifferent Europe," wrote the Duc de Broglie in his book *The King's Secret*, in which he called the partition an "act of brigandage." [5] Voltaire sent his congratulations to Frederick the Great, praising him for his political tact and knowledge. Many contemporary statesmen not only considered the partition a fortunate event which saved Europe from war but also believed that the firm and spirited intervention of Prussia and Austria prevented Poland from becoming a Russian province and that the partition was really a defeat for Catherine. [6]

A notable exception to this attitude of indifference was Thomas Jefferson. Far across the seas the partition of 1795 and especially the failure of Thaddeus Kosciuszko's rebellion of 1794 affected him deeply. It was perhaps his lifelong friendship with Kosciuszko, who had taken such a heroic part in the American Revolution, that moved the famous Virginian to denounce the partition as a "crime and atrocity." From this time on many Americans, influenced by Jefferson's attitude but failing to examine the history of the partition, have given repeated evidence of this feeling. [7]

The Poles themselves were not shocked at the partition of their country. Many of them deplored it; a great majority seemed to welcome it. Thousands of Greek-Orthodox Poles were elated to find themselves under the rule of Greek-Orthodox Russia. The Polish gentry in Galicia celebrated their incorporation into the Austrian Empire with feasting. [8] According to Professor W.

3. *Ibid.*

4. *Ibid.*

5. Duc de Broglie, *The King's Secret—The Secret Correspondence of Louis XV with His Diplomatic Agents* (London, 1881), *1*, 68 ff.

6. Horn, *British Public Opinion*, p. 46.

7. Thomas Jefferson changed his mind a few months after his denunciation of the partitions. In a letter to one of his friends he wrote: "I have been reading Komorzewski's *Coup d'Oeil* on the history of Poland . . . it gives a lesson which all our countrymen should study; the example of a country erased from the map of the world by the dissensions of its own citizens." See Andrew A. Lipsomb and Albert E. Bergh, eds., *The Writings of Thomas Jefferson* (Washington, GPO, 1903), *18*, 161 and *13*, 66.

8. Henryk Frankel, *Poland: The Struggle for Power, 1772–1939* (London, L. Drummond, 1946), p. 30.

Tokarz, "the Galician gentry after the Partition asked only for religion, property, the punishment of the apostate with death and confiscation of his estates, and the prevention of nobles living outside Galicia from acquiring estates there." [9] When the Austrian monarch in 1782 relieved the peasants of some feudal burdens and divided up some land among them, the majority of the Galician peasants were lost to the national cause. For centuries the Polish masters had treated the peasants like animals, had beaten, oppressed and humiliated them. Now a foreign master brought them relief. "It is not surprising, therefore," Henryk Frankel wrote, "that during the whole of the nineteenth century Polish peasants used to say 'Our Emperor—Franz Joseph.' " [10] For a long time those Polish nationals who became Prussian subjects also fared better under that rule. As a matter of fact, Hans Kohn concluded, the Poles appeared to be better subjects of Prussia than the Germans.[11] Early observers noted the desire of many a Pole to be an Austrian, a Prussian, a Frenchman, or a Russian. These desires became a reality in 1795.[12]

Many sincerely patriotic Poles considered the first partition a blessing, an event which might lead to the necessary reforms within the country and to the strengthening of the government. This hope was based on the realistic and careful counsel of Jean Jacques Rousseau. Poland, he wrote in 1771, would probably be "devoured," but if she wanted to continue her existence she must see to it that she was not "digested." His emphatic advice was "Get rid of your traditions which have made you what you are." [13]

Had the Poles carried out Rousseau's suggestion, the first partition really might have been a blessing in disguise. But the political and social traditions of the Poles which made their country politically impotent and backward were too deeply imbedded in their nature to be changed quickly and easily. In the face of Poland's history before and after the partition one cannot but realize that the partition was not an "act of brigandage" but a natural denouement of two centuries of lawlessness, anarchy, and irresponsible rule of nobles who had "plenty of diamonds but no linen."

Within a generation the critical, realistic 18th-century atti-

9. Quoted by Frankel, pp. 30–1.
10. *Ibid.*, p. 75.
11. Hans Kohn, *The Idea of Nationalism* (New York, 1944), p. 203.
12. William Coxe, *Travels in Poland, Russia, Sweden and Denmark* (London, 1802), p. 13.
13. Vaughan, *Political Writings of Rousseau, 2,* 442–3.

tude began to change. It was reflected in the often-quoted lines of Thomas Campbell, "Hope, for a season, bade the world farewell, and Freedom shriek'd as Kosciuszko fell." [14] To 19th-century historians and intellectuals the partition of Poland became an "act of brigandage," a notorious example of international immorality. Influenced by the liberalism of the 19th century, the friends of Poland, who mostly belonged to the extreme liberal school of politics, began to press history into their service and torture her into proving that Europe had to erase her "bad conscience" by bringing Poland back into the family of nations.[15] Historical views invented by the Polish emigrants in days when few were competent to contradict them were reasserted. To some extent in England, but still more generally in France, the old controversy of the partitions was reopened. By outright inversion of the real degrees of responsibility the chief blame was laid on autocratic Russia. Prussia, however, was looked upon as a pitiful and subordinate accomplice, while Austria was practically absolved as an unwilling accessory. During the first World War, while Russia was still an ally of the Western Powers, many prominent Poles and their friends began to change history again to suit their needs. At that time Prussia became the chief instigator of the partitions, and Russia was almost completely absolved of responsibility.[16]

Failure of the Polish revolts of 1830, 1848, and 1863 did not change the attitude of Western liberals. Had they examined the causes for the rapid defeat of the Polish revolutionary forces they would have seen that after the partitions the majority of the Polish people, including the members of the nobility, had become faithful subjects of the partitioning powers so that the call to arms found the mass of the people inactive. The peasants upon whom depended the success of the revolutionists suspected aristocratic aims in the uprising of the Polish nobles, and on many occasions showed "a hos-

14. Thomas Campbell, *Works* (London, 1851), p. 14.
15. Examples of such works are Duc de Broglie, *The King's Secret;* Lord Eversley, *The Partitions of Poland* (New York, 1915); Robert H. Lord, *The Second Partition of Poland* (Cambridge, Mass., 1915); E. H. Lewinski-Corwin, *The Political History of Poland* (New York, 1917); Stanislaw Filasiewicz, ed., *La Question polonaise pendant la guerre mondiale: Récueil des actes diplomatiques, traités et documents concernant la Pologne* (Paris, Comité National Polonaise, 1918); Miecislaus Haiman, *The Fall of Poland in Contemporary American Opinion* (Chicago, 1935). See also Karl Marx and Friedrich Engels, *Selected Correspondence 1846–1895* (New York, International Publishers, 1942).
16. See Ignace Jan Paderewski, "Poland's So-called Corridor," *Foreign Affairs, 11* (1933), 421.

tile attitude and sometimes threw themselves on the insurgents and bound them." [17] The attitude of the magnates was also unfavorable. This is seen in Adam Mickiewicz's testimony: "Men who have killed the Polish Revolution [were] the Czartoryskis, the Zamoyskis. . . . Count Zamoyski had related that his friends and he, seeing no better way of forestalling the revolution of 29th November, 1830 than by increasing the vigilance of the Russian police, left in the apartment of the Grand Duke Constantine an anonymous letter which denounced the plans of the conspirators." [18] No wonder that when the revolution finally broke out in February 1831 it was speedily crushed by the overwhelming power of Russia, and the vanquished remnants of the revolutionists were forced to leave the country.

The revolutions of 1848 in Europe again provided a favorable opportunity for patriotic Poles to recover independence for their country. Public opinion, however, was divided. The peasantry, remembering the past, feared a return to slavery if Poland again became independent, while a large number of nobles preferred to serve the Prussians, Russians, and Austrians.[19] When the revolution did break out, the Russian army under the leadership of Prince Paskevitch and the Polish Count Rzewuski quelled the insurrection with little trouble.

The insurrection of 1863, like those of 1830 and 1848, failed for lack of popular support. After that the Polish people abhorred the idea of another rising. Even the soldierly spirit, once predominant in Poland, became less and less conspicuous. "Among the rank and file, even of the town population," Dyboski wrote, "the idea of a struggle for national reunion and deliverance had tended to become dormant, and the slogan of a reborn free Poland was only used rhetorically on holiday occasions in self-governing Austrian Poland, where such demonstrations were possible." [20]

Elsewhere the failure of the insurrection and the Russian atrocities that followed it aroused public opinion. In most of the

17. Bronislaw Limanowski, *Powstanie 1863-4* (Insurrection of 1863-4) (Lwow, 1892), p. 57. Roman Dyboski wrote: ". . . neither the first nor the second insurrection succeeded in reaching that bed-rock of Polish national strength—the peasant class." See Roman Dyboski, *Outlines of Polish History* (London, Allen and Unwin, 1931), p. 198.
18. Quoted by Frankel, *Poland,* p. 37.
19. Limanowski, *Powstanie 1863-4,* pp. 370-1.
20. Roman Dyboski, "The Polish Question during the World War," in W. F. Reddaway, ed., *The Cambridge History of Poland, 1697-1935* (New York, Cambridge University Press, 1941), p. 461.

European capitals and even in the United States [21] Polish exiles gave exaggerated accounts of Polish patriotism. The picture of the romantic, patriotic, and aristocratic Pole became imprinted on the European imagination. The emigration of Poles after 1831 stimulated discussion in academic circles. Books and articles began to appear glorifying Polish patriotism and at the same time stigmatizing the partition of Poland as a "great Russian crime." At a time when the exiled Poles could no longer be taken as representatives of the new age, they became the prime and almost the only source of the many works and articles written about Poland.[22]

To the 19th-century historians and intellectuals Poland, in spite of her internal weakness, became a focal area of the international "left-wing" campaign against autocratic Russia; to their successors, the 20th-century historians, Poland became the strategic area of the international "right-wing" campaign against Soviet Russia. This 20th-century fear of Bolshevism, combined with ignorance of internal Polish political realities, produced a curiously distorted picture of Poland as a heroic little nation long struggling to be free and democratic.

21. See Miecislaus Haiman, *The Fall of Poland in Contemporary American Opinion.*

22. One of the contemporary statesmen who saw the fallacy of the popular interpretation of the Polish partitions was the Marquess of Salisbury. In 1863 he wrote: "If they [men of contemporary Europe] had been watching the relations of the Poles and Russians for centuries, as they had watched those of the French and Germans, they would probably have taken a different view of the moral aspect of the affair. They would have seen that the conquest was but a re-conquest; that the transactions that were passing before their eyes were but the closing scene of a long and varied drama; and that the mass of inhabitants of the annexed provinces, far from being robbed of their freedom and their country, were only being re-united to those of their own race and their own religion from whom the ambition of the Polish nobles had severed them for so long." Marquess of Salisbury, "Poland," *Quarterly Review, 113* (London, 1863), 11.

2. The Rebirth of Poland: a Historical Miracle

> *Seigneur, donnez-nous la guerre*
> *universelle qui délivrera Pologne.*
> *Adam Mickiewicz (1832)*

ADAM MICKIEWICZ, the greatest Polish poet and patriot, recognizing after the failure of the Polish Revolution of 1830 the futility of future insurrections, wrote a poem calculated to strengthen the hearts of the distracted Polish exiles. This poem, later often to be quoted by Paderewski, called upon God to grant the Poles a universal war which would bring Poland back into the family of nations. Written in the form of a prayer, it asked:

> For a universal war for the freedom of nations
> We beseech Thee, O Lord.
> For national arms and eagles
> We beseech Thee, O Lord.
> For the independence, integrity and freedom of our country
> We beseech Thee, O Lord.[1]

As the 19th century was drawing to a close, it seemed that only the fulfillment of Mickiewicz's prayer could resurrect Poland. France, once an ally of Poland, was weak and drawing closer to tsarist Russia for security. Austria, which had given her Poles self-government, was drifting into greater dependency on her powerful German ally. Germany herself, growing more and more sure of her own power and destiny, was continuing to repress Polish national feeling. In Russia the policy of Russification was meeting with greater and greater success.

Not only did the Poles in the three partitioned sections diverge widely from each other, but the generation growing up since the last armed struggle of 1863 had become too absorbed in the pursuit of material ends to retain any vivid sense of national reality.

1. Private papers of Edward M. House, in the House Collection of the Yale University Library. From the copy of Paderewski's speech in America in the autumn of 1916.

7

The Polish aristocracy and the landed gentry followed a policy of reconciliation with their respective partitioners, which Dyboski called a "three-fold loyalty." This practice of *trojalism* became the dominating principle of Polish life. Without necessarily meaning complete assimilation, it did involve the acceptance by the Poles of the forms of private and public life prevailing in each of the partitioned parts of Poland. "In effect," W. J. Rose wrote, "it meant that Poles would remain, even speaking their own tongue and enjoying certain of their own institutions; but that *Poland* would cease to be, not only as a name on the map, but as an idea and ideal in the minds of its people." [2]

The peasantry, nationally unawakened, unpatriotic, always conservative in thought and deed, always fanatic, bent on acquiring more and more land and wealth, could not be expected to pursue what seemed to them a chimerical policy of national reunion and freedom. Their relative simplicity and isolation made it hardly possible for them to understand more general political problems. Communal self-government allowed, within certain limits, the settlement of most of the problems of everyday life, leaving the large problems of state—law, military service, taxes, schools, official language, means of communication, prices of natural and manufactured products—to be regulated by some superior and undetermined authority. The peasant's attitude toward them "was more or less like his attitude toward the weather—fundamentally passive resignation, with sometimes an attempt to influence with prayer or gift the powers in their treatment of the individual's own sphere of interest." [3] Although Polish peasants were individualistic, giving an impression of independence, they shunned revolt and violence. "The belief that he [the peasant] can rule his own life," Sula Benet wrote, "is rooted in the conviction that despite any fate or any oppressor, he can rule himself." [4] The peasants resembled the Polish nobility—proud, domineering, often arrogant—but at the same time they would humble themselves before their lords and benefactors. History testifies that there were no significant peasant revolts in Poland.

The main reason for the submissiveness of the peasantry—

2. W. J. Rose, "Russian Poland in the Later Nineteenth Century," in Reddaway, *Cambridge History of Poland*, p. 392.

3. William I. Thomas and Florian Znaniecki, *The Polish Peasant in Europe and America* (New York, Knopf, 1927), *1*, 332.

4. Sula Benet, *Song, Dance and Customs of Peasant Poland* (New York, Roy Publishers, 1952), p. 19.

yielding to authority after only slight pressure or a faint-hearted struggle—seems to have been, and perhaps still is, the Roman Catholic influence which has shaped the peasants' attitude of non-aggression. The church taught them for centuries to depend on Divine Providence rather than on independent action or thinking. At the outbreak of the first World War the concepts of equality, of mutual assistance, of sharing, and of taking risks in patriotic revolts were not sufficiently active in the peasants to make them want to participate in a struggle for national reunion and freedom.

Nor was the Polish national struggle, if such it may be called, as popular among the peasantry as the determined struggles for liberation in other European countries were among the first generation of industrial workers, who had been recruited from the peasants. The era of serfdom was still fresh in the Polish peasants' memories and they feared losing advantages gained in the 19th century should Poland again become independent. They were still under the influence of peasant traditions, were usually bitter, were riddled with conflicts and disordered personalities, and were far from liberal, patriotic, or socially altruistic.[5]

The industrial workers who were not tied to the soil or to peasant traditions were more advanced, more cohesive, and freer of traditional bonds. They were more gregarious and socially minded, but not all of them were won over by patriotic appeals. Some condemned outright any sign of chauvinism or patriotism, while others entered freely into the ranks of Polish patriotic groups. To the former, patriotism was only a mask to cover the egoistic aims of the gentry and bourgeoisie. They saw no hope in insurrection as an instrument for Polish independence.[6]

Only the intelligentsia of the towns had kept the torch of national aspiration burning. Though they had been devoured by the partitioning powers, they did not allow themselves to be completely digested. But they were irrevocably divided between two contemporary European currents: socialism and nationalism. Soon the two groups lost their homogeneity and split into antagonistic factions, bitterly contending against each other, thus undermining their own strength.

During the whole history of Poland under partition only a

5. *Ibid.*, p. 32.
6. See Ignace Daszynski, *Polityka Proletariatu* (Warsaw, 1907), pp. 28, 89, and 97; also Casimir Dluski, *Rownosc* (Geneva, 1880), and Frankel, *Poland*, pp. 66–7.

small minority of Poles worked for the re-establishment of a Polish state. This group was composed of Polish exiles, lesser nobility, some industrial workers, and impoverished gentry who were forced to enter the ranks of the proletariat but never lost their hope of salvation and return to their former position of prestige, wealth, and power. Long before the "internationalists" divided into pro-Luxemburgians and pro-Leninites,[7] this "nationalist" group split into two factions: Idealists and Realists. These differed as to the methods that ought to be pursued as well as to the ends. Not long before the first World War both factions split again into various antagonistic subdivisions.

The Idealists were the members of the Polish Socialist party (PPS). Its main strength lay in Russian Poland, where it had to operate illegally until 1905 and again after 1907. At the outset the party stressed the necessity of both national and social freedom. Some of its leaders emphasized the nationalist aspect and considered the Socialist propaganda of the party a weapon by which to gain independence without prejudicing the future economic and social system of Poland. Others gave equal importance to both aspects of the party's program. After 1905 the PPS split into two groups, the Left Socialist wing and the "right" or "Revolutionary" faction. The first, under the leadership of Ignace Daszynski, aimed not at complete independence for Poland but at wide autonomy within a Russian republic, and meanwhile favored cooperation with the Russian Socialist movement. The second, eventually taken over by Joseph Pilsudski, can claim credit with some justification for the re-establishment of Poland. The members of the right wing were ardent patriots and nationalists. Their patriotism, however, was influenced by an abstract and impractical romanticism. Both factions believed that any future independent Poland could not avoid being Socialist and that therefore the struggle for independence was synonymous with the struggle for socialism.

Socialist action and propaganda achieved little. Pilsudski, leader of the right wing of the PPS, began to pin his hopes on war rather than on insurrection as the lever which might send the Russian Empire to its doom. During the Russo-Japanese war he went to Tokyo to propose to the Japanese military authorities that Poland should be armed behind Russia's back. He also visited a number of Polish notables in German and Austrian Poland, Lithuania, Ukraine, and Russia and tried to incite them to action.

7. See below, pp. 28–37.

Everywhere he met with excuses and objections. He was even denounced to the police. Roman Dmowski, head of the National Democratic party (ND or Endeks) and hence Paderewski's superior in authority, went to the length of following Pilsudski to Japan to convince the Japanese that Pilsudski in no way represented Poland. By 1914 Pilsudski himself began to doubt whether Poland could ever be resurrected.

Dmowski considered that if the existence of the Polish nation were threatened in the future it would be not from Russia but from Germany.[8] His party, which had been formed in Russian Poland in the 1870's, drew its strength from three main sources. The first was the infiltration of secular currents from Western Europe: the realism of Comte and the general implications of Darwinism, which convinced the Poles of the futility of romantic yearning and of the inevitability implied in the doctrine of survival of the fittest. The second source was the powerful economic argument. The process of industrialization, with the marked growth of city life, was moving swiftly eastward in Europe, bringing with it affluence and a high standard of living. To many Polish industrialists and workers such progress offered a great opportunity to cast in their lot with tsarist Russia, where after 1871 prosperity was opening up markets as far away as eastern Siberia. Cherishing their vigorous economy, they were at all times fearful of revolution or war. The final source was Polish clericalism, which was characterized by reliance on divine power, by fatalism, submission, expectation of miracles, hope, and day dreams rather than action. The clergy, as part of the intelligentsia, followed the traditional principle of "church before state." Their teaching and activity were aimed primarily at controlling the people and securing the welfare of the church rather than at re-establishing an independent Poland.[9]

From its birth the Polish National Democratic party was supported by the Russian Government, not so much because it was openly pro-Russian as because its conservative program often helped the government to carry out reactionary measures. Having abandoned the idea of any struggle for the independence of Poland, the National Democrats determined to live on good terms with the Russian antidemocratic government. Instead of supporting the revolution of 1905 in Poland they openly opposed it. "Even Polish leaders, such as Dmowski, Lednicki; the brothers Grabski,

8. Roman Dmowski, *La Question polonaise* (Paris, A. Colin, 1909), pp. 306–7.
9. Frankel, *Poland,* pp. 68–9.

Harusiewicz . . . as well as the Polish representatives in the Imperial Council, such as Skirmunt and Korwin-Milewski," Korostovetz wrote, "had . . . no conception of Poland as an independent State, and in their discussions expressed far more moderate opinions on Polish national aspirations than the Russian *intelligentsia* and their representatives in the Imperial Duma." [10] Roman Dmowski believed that Russia would no longer be capable of returning to an effective anti-Polish policy: "She has, and she will have, too many difficulties external as well as internal in her empire; her political organism is too disturbed and too weakened for any such system to become possible, however evil the intentions of successive governments." [11] Thus when the war came he called upon the Polish people in Poland to rally to the tsar's army. [12] The Endeks had as their main program "unification of Poland under the sceptre of the Russian monarchy." The implication of this policy was far-reaching. It meant abjuring any political activity or use of violence. It simply meant accepting subjection to Russia, and to other empires as well. The leaders of the party were the high clergy and the great Polish landowners, including among others Count Zamoyski, Prince Sapieha, and Prince Czartoryski. The more prominent members were Roman Dmowski, official head of the ND, and Ignace Jan Paderewski.

Dmowski was a biologist by profession. It was his early scientific training and education in biology that had made him a Realist and Darwinian in politics. He prided himself on never having been a "preacher of liberal humanitarian principles" and never having belonged to any of the international organizations founded for increasing the happiness of mankind. [13] Throughout his career he always collaborated with Russia, "arguing that a victory of the latter over Germany (with the aid of Western Democracies) would mean the uniting of Polish land under the sceptre of the Tsar." [14] Thus, when Pilsudski and others were working for revolution in 1905, Dmowski opposed them with all his power.

Dmowski's foreign policy and political Darwinism may be

10. Vladimir K. Korostovetz, *The Re-Birth of Poland* (London, Bles, 1928), pp. 15–16.

11. Dmowski, *La Question polonaise*, pp. 306–7.

12. Frankel, *Poland*, p. 79.

13. Roman Dmowski, *Polityka Polska i Odbudowanie Panstwa* (*Polish Politics and the Restoration of the State*) (Warsaw, Parzynski i Niklewicz, 1925), p. 139.

14. W. J. Rose, "Russian Poland in the Later Nineteenth Century," in Reddaway, *Cambridge History of Poland*, p. 398.

judged further from his own prolific writings. In *Thoughts of a Modern Pole* he set down an elaborate philosophy of racial combat.[15] The Germans who tried to Germanize the Poles of Posen by force, Dmowski wrote, were only obeying the supreme summons and sanctions of their race loyalty and race destiny. An equal aspiration to loyalty and to destiny should characterize the Poles. "Healthy nations endeavor to denationalize other nations." It is a weakness, he continued, when Poles vote for a Ruthenian high school in Galicia for the Ruthenians. "The fate of the Ruthenians is to remain within the boundaries of Poland—and they should, when occasion arises, be Polonized." [16] On the basis of this philosophy the members of Dmowski's party demanded at the Peace Conference in 1919 that Poland should include a great assortment of territories that were not Polish at all.

The National Democratic party, like all other Polish parties and groups, did not retain its homogeneity for long. Toward the end of 1912 there took place at Cracow a reunion of the representatives of the National Democratic party from the three parts of Poland. Here the Realists divided into three groups: pro-Russian, pro-Austrian, and pro-German. Dmowski, leader of the pro-Russian group, opened the conference by saying: "The victory of Germany would necessarily have as its first consequence that the Kingdom [Russian Poland] would be taken away from Russia . . . Prussia would under no circumstance consent to abandon it to Austria. . . . From this point of view, in the face of a possible Austro-Russian conflict, and under present circumstances, the anti-Russian attitude cannot be considered nationally desirable." He finished his address by heaping scorn on the Cracow Conservatives with their Austrian "orientation." "Berlin alone," he said convincingly, "will dictate the terms of any peace in case of victory of the Central Powers. At best the defeat of Russia would only mean a fresh partition of Poland. . . . Polish policy should favor the Russian cause in any struggle. . . ." [17]

The pro-Austrians sought support in Austria because she had made possible a normal development of the national culture among

15. *Mysli Nowoczesnego Polaka* (Lwow, 1893).

16. *Ibid.*, p. 45.

17. *Memorjal Romana Dmowskiego, odczytany na Konferencji politykow polskich w trzech dzielnic w Krakowie pod koniec r. 1912.* (The address of Roman Dmowski, read at the Cracow Conference of Polish political leaders from the three partitioned parts of Poland at the end of 1912.) See Marjan Seyda, *Polska na Przelomie Wiekow* (*Poland at the Crossroads of History*) (Posen, 1927), *1*, 531–4.

one part of the Polish people. They put no faith at all in the promises of Russia; and their conclusion was that self-government for Poland was quite incompatible with the despotism of the tsars. The Galician Realists, men like Bobrzynski, Jaworski, and Bilinski, therefore advocated an Austrophile policy. The most for which this group hoped was the union of all Russian Poland with the whole of Galicia and the transformation of Austria-Hungary into a triple monarchy.

The pro-German Polish group based its hopes on some Austro-German agreement which would give national autonomy to the Poles in Germany and Austria. Their policy was similar to that of the pro-Austrian group to which they looked for guidance.

No matter which Realist policy won out, whether the pro-Russian, pro-German, or pro-Austrian, the Poles would not have seen the unification of Polish lands or the independence of their country.

In 1914 war broke out. At first it held little promise for Polish independence. "On the outbreak of war," Count Burian wrote, "when all the great European interests came into conflict nobody gave a thought to Poland. It did not seem desirable or necessary to any of the three powers concerned in the partition to disturb the Polish problem." [18] It was only when the United States entered the conflict, making it a world war, that the triple defeat, for which some Poles were hoping, became possible. Mickiewicz's prayer was answered with the intervention of the New World, for the first time, in the affairs of the Old. The miracle became confirmed and personified in Woodrow Wilson, a man who knew little about Poland even after the United States joined the European conflict. Perhaps it was his consciousness of being a "miracle man" that prompted him to say to Paderewski on the eve of his election on November 6, 1916: "My dear Paderewski, I can tell that Poland will be resurrected and will exist again. For Poland this miracle of independence will come from the West . . ." [19]

THE CENTRAL POWERS AND THE
POLISH QUESTION

The outbreak of the first World War divided the Polish people into many antagonistic groups. None envisaged a fully independ-

---

18. Count Stephan Burian, *Austria in Dissolution* (London, Doran, 1925), p. 78.
19. Rom Landau, *Ignace Paderewski, Musician and Statesman* (New York, Thomas Y. Crowell, 1934), p. 115.

ent Poland. "Nobody believed or worked," Paderewski declared, "for an independent Poland before the outbreak of the war and during the first years of the war." [20] During the four years of the war the Poles were actually fighting each other, insofar as they were fighting at all, without the slightest chance of recovering their freedom by their own exertions. "None of the Poles engaged in the various armies," Korostovetz wrote, "had ever dreamt of any political independence, extending beyond national autonomy and territorial home rule." [21] Joseph Pilsudski, future dictator of Poland, acknowledged these facts.[22]

Immediately after the outbreak of the war Pilsudski, who more than any other Polish leader was aware of the opportunities that the conflict offered to Poland, announced his pro-Austrian policy and began to seek allies in Austria. At first he found full support for the formation of a Polish legion in Austrian Poland to be used in the war against Russia. The Poles of the Dual Empire were well organized. They preferred Austria to Russia, for she treated them with indulgence, owing primarily to the decisive position which their deputies held in the Reichsrath.[23] "The Poles," Cruttwell wrote, "though far from enthusiastic soldiers, caused the rulers of Austria-Hungary little serious uneasiness. It was far otherwise," he continued, "with Czechs and Slovaks and the southern Slavs." [24] In Galicia there already existed some semimilitary organizations

20. Ignace Jan Paderewski, "Helpless Poland," *Independent, 83* (1915), 192.
21. Korostovetz, *The Re-Birth of Poland*, p. 49.
22. In 1931 Pilsudski wrote: "I am repeatedly astonished that such simple truths and historical facts are continuously twisted and continuously falsified. For there is no doubt whatsoever that at the outbreak of the war in 1914 the Poles and Poland were in a state of complete prostration and complete impotence. It is then an incontestible fact that in each of the dismembered parts all of the Poles did what their partitioning powers ordered. . . . This fact is so true and incontrovertible that it is with genuine displeasure that one sees or hears it denied by those who glorify themselves, and themselves only, in their accounts of all they have done." Jozef Pilsudski, *Poprawki Historyczne (Historical Corrections)* (Warsaw, Instytut Badania Najnowszej Historji Polski, 1931), pp. 7-8.
23. In the last years before the war many Polish aristocrats had high offices in the Austro-Hungarian Empire. Leon Bilinski was at the Treasury, as was W. Korytowski in 1907 and W. Zaleski in 1913. From 1895 to 1898 K. Badeni was prime minister, and at the turn of the century Goluchowski was minister of foreign affairs. Poles were also ministers of education and communication. Moreover in every cabinet from 1873 to 1914 there was a "minister for Galicia," usually an eminent member of the Polish Parliamentary Club in Vienna. All of them served the dynasty "without conditions." See A. J. P. Taylor, *The Hapsburg Monarchy, 1809–1918* (London, 1948), p. 99.
24. C. R. M. F. Cruttwell, *A History of the Great War, 1914–1918* (2d ed. Oxford, Oxford University Press, 1936), p. 49.

(*sokols*), which Austria hoped to use in case of a conflict with Russia over Balkan problems, under the leadership of the future Polish General Haller; and rifle societies, consisting of conservative elements under the command of Januszajtis. Pilsudski's contribution was the creation of a new organization, consisting of Socialist workers, called the Union of Riflemen. The societies were non-political in form, though most of them had definite political leanings and of course depended to a great extent on official Austrian sanction and support. The future General Sikorski, engaged in organizing student circles for military training, also allied himself with Pilsudski who, in a short time, succeeded in uniting all the Polish military groups in Austria under his leadership. It was in the military movement in Galicia that nearly all those who later became leaders of the Polish Army, including General Sosnkowski, Rydz-Smigly, Kukiel, Skladkowski and others, received their training.

Joseph Pilsudski counted on the general upheaval following the outbreak of the war to realize his dream of an independent Poland, or at least of the union of Russian Poland with Austrian Poland under an autonomous regime. He succeeded in convincing Austria that it would be to her advantage to recognize Polish aspirations; she would then be able to appeal to the Russian Poles to join the Polish legions of Pilsudski and thus fortify her military position.

Soon after the war began the Supreme Command of the German and Austrian armies issued a manifesto which told the Poles they were being brought liberty, tolerance, and respect for a religion so "terribly oppressed" by the Russians. With our flags, it continued, "come freedom and independence for you." [25]

Immediately after this proclamation the Polish Club in the Austrian parliament declared that the hour had struck for which three generations of the Polish people had shed their blood vainly in a terrible and hopeless struggle with the Russian invaders. The same Poles who had hitherto blamed Austria and Germany for their part in the partition of Poland now openly stated that Austria, in defense of the liberty of the Poles and other peoples, was sending to Poland a "mighty army against the Russian oppressors"—the enemy of mankind.[26]

25. Kazimierz Kumaniecki, *Odbudowa Panstwowosci Polskiej; Najwazniejsze Dokumenty, 1912–1924* (*The Restoration of the Polish State; The Most Important Documents*) (Warsaw, Czernecki, 1924), p. 25.

26. This declaration stated: "The Virtuous Emperor of this State, under whose

A significant event occurred in Vienna on August 22, 1914, which clearly demonstrated the situation of the Polish "Austrophiles." On that day the emperor approved a draft of a manifesto which was drawn up by Leon Bilinski, finance minister of the Austro-Hungarian Monarchy and one of the outstanding leaders of the Polish Club. This manifesto, which revealed the policy of the Austrian Poles, read as follows: "If Almighty God gives victory to the Allied Armies, *your country shall be incorporated among my States for ever*, in such a way that together with my territory inhabited by your compatriots it shall form a unified Kingdom of Poland, the administration of which I shall entrust— subject to the best interests and needs of the Monarchy as a whole —to a national Government responsible to the Diet at Warsaw." [27] The Crown Council at the behest of Count Tisza rejected this manifesto.

Not everybody shared the views of the Polish Club. At first the Austrian and German pro-Polish statements were calculated to win over the Polish masses in Russian-occupied Poland. As soon as the Germans and Austrians began to win on the Russian front, their interest in the Poles cooled considerably.

As the hold of the German and Austrian armies over the occupied area of Poland grew stronger, the plans of the Central Powers became clearer. Austria and Germany would probably have denounced their previous proclamations which promised Polish "independence" had it not been for the problem of manpower. The Germans could not afford to keep large occupying forces in Poland at a time when the western front demanded more and more men. But neither could they conscript Poles into the German Army for occupation duties without contravening a principle of international law laid down at the Hague Conference of 1907 against mobilizing armed forces within occupied areas in wartime. And

---

just and wise government a part of our nation for half a century was able to develop Polish national forces, is entering the struggle for the highest ideals of human culture, and looks upon the Polish nation as a proven defender of these ideals. . . . Under Polish Command and in close alliance with the Supreme Command of the Austrian and Hungarian army, the Polish legions will go into battle so that, in this greatest of wars, they should make a contribution worthy of the Polish nation which will be a pledge for a better future. Submit with confidence and complete faith to the leadership of the Polish Club. . . ." *Ibid.*, pp. 16–17.

27. According to Smogorzewski, Tisza rejected this because he felt that "after such a manifesto the Emperor could not again resume personal and diplomatic relations with the Tsar." Tisza, concludes Smogorzewski, wished to avoid "any irreparable diplomatic breach which would hinder a separate peace in the East between the Central Powers and Russia." Casimir Smogorzewski, *Poland's Access to the Sea* (London, Allen and Unwin, 1934), p. 113.

conscription of a willing population promised better results than compulsory incorporation of thousands of Poles into German and Austrian armies. It was therefore decided, contrary to previous declarations, to create an independent Polish kingdom, under the protection of, and allied with, the Central Powers. In order to avoid dissension between the Austrian and German governments —for there was considerable difference of opinion as to who should administer the occupied areas, Austria desiring Warsaw against Germany's wish, which prevailed—it was agreed to set up a Polish state in the occupied part of Russia only. On November 5, 1916, the following manifesto was published simultaneously in Berlin and Vienna:

> . . . His Majesty the German Emperor and His Majesty the Austrian Emperor and Apostolic King of Hungary, sustained by their firm confidence in the final victory of their arms, and guided by the wish to lead to a happy future the Polish districts which by their brave armies were snatched with heavy sacrifices from Russian power, have agreed to form from these districts an independent state with an hereditary monarchy and a Constitution. The more precise regulation of the frontiers of the Kingdom of Poland remains reserved. In union with both Allied Powers the new Kingdom will find the guarantees, which it desires for the free development of its strength. In its own army the glorious traditions of the Polish Army of frontier times and the memory of our brave Polish fellow-combatants in the great war of the present time will continue to live. Its organization, training and command will be regulated by mutual agreement.[28]

In conjunction with this manifesto Generals von Beseler and von Kuk, German and Austrian commanders of the occupied areas of Russian Poland, published a proclamation which asked the Poles to support the new state by enlisting in their armies, so that the future Polish kingdom might become a reality. The appeal read as follows:

> The struggle with Russia has not yet ended; in this struggle you must also participate. Stand by our side therefore as volunteers and help us to crown our victory against your oppressor. Your brothers in the Polish legions fought with us courageously and gloriously; follow in their footsteps and enlist in

28. *New York Times,* Nov. 6, 1916.

the new formations which, united with the legions, will constitute the Polish Army, which will provide strong support for
your new state and will secure its safety both within and without. . . .[29]

To carry out these demands a Provisional Council of State was
formed with Pilsudski as a military member.[30] The response of the
Polish population was negligible; only a few thousand men enlisted
in the army.[31]

This policy of the Central Powers continued without any major
alteration until March 1917, when the Russian Revolution brought
a fundamental change in the situation. Germany then became
nervous. Whereas in the early days of her occupation the Poles
had been friendly to her, their allegiance now passed over to the
new Russia. The Polish legions were no longer prepared to fight
the Russians.[32] Many of the members were pro-Bolshevik, and
even those who held no political opinion were swayed by the early
Bolshevik pro-Polish declarations. Austria and Germany quickly
became aware of this political change in the legions and, to eliminate undesirable elements, demanded an oath of allegiance to the
German and Austrian emperors. Pilsudski himself was imprisoned
in the fortress of Magdeburg, from which he was released by the
German revolution on November 10, 1918. Those who escaped
imprisonment formed the illegal Polish military organization
(POW) which, commanded by the future Marshal Smigly-Rydz,
organized sabotage in the rear of the German and Austrian armies.
Some legionnaires, however, under the command of General Haller
and others, continued to fight on the side of Austria and Germany.
The Provisional Council of State, which was succeeded in September 1917 by the Council of Regency, together with the Polish Club
in the Vienna parliament and its representatives in the Austrian
Government, continued their cooperation with the Central Powers
until the defeat.

Even after the Western Allies had declared their intention to
create an independent Polish state, the Polish Parliamentary Club

29. Filasiewicz, *La Question polonaise*, p. 66. See also Kumaniecki, *Odbudowa*,
p. 50.

30. *Ibid.*, p. 72.

31. Marshal von Hindenburg, *Out of My Life* (London, Cassell and Co., 1920),
pp. 222–4.

32. *Papers Relating to the Foreign Relations of the United States: 1917* (3
vols. Washington, GPO, 1942) Supplement 2, *2*, 256. Hereafter cited as *FR*.

and its counterparts in Austrian Poland remained pro-Austrian.[33] On June 3, 1918, in a "strictly confidential" memorandum of the Polish Club addressed to the Austrian Government, the Austrian Poles, looking forward to an independent kingdom under the Hapsburg Monarchy, reasserted "their unchanging attachment and gratitude to the most noble Emperor," and promised to "remain faithful and steadfast to their tacit agreement of August 1914." [34] Not only did they support the Central Powers but they also declared their "readiness to support the Germans against the efforts of the Czechs to set up a Czechoslovak state . . . and against those Slovenes who aim to set up a Yugoslav state." [35]

German policy toward Poland resembled that of Austria. Yet the German Poles did not exert as much pressure on the German Government as did the Austrian Poles on the Austrian. They continued to support the German emperor but, unlike the Polish group in Austria which supported the Central Powers until the end of the war, they withdrew their support a few months before the Armistice.[36] According to the German minister, Erzberger,

> the wishes of the Polish population in Prussia were modest; they aimed in general at the recognition of equal rights for the Polish and German languages, and in particular for the inclusion of Polish in religious instructions. . . . I was in close contact with several influential Polish leaders; there were numerous conferences with them. . . . However, in 1918, the Polish Club in the Reichstag finally voted against the granting of new war credits, an action which was most deeply regretted by the more right-wing Poles.[37]

Field Marshal von Hindenburg and General Ludendorff explained, after the end of the war, the reasons behind the policy of

33. *FR: 1918*, Supplement 1, p. 339.
34. Leon Bilinski, *Wspomnienia i Dokumenty, 1846–1922 (Memoirs and Documents)* (Warsaw, Hoesick, 1924–25), *2*, 412.
35. *Ibid.*
36. Czartoryski wrote as follows on the attitude of the Russian Poles toward the war: "They discharged without exception and willingly their duty as Prussian citizens and marched out joyfully to fight for Kaiser and Reich in the East and West . . . for the Poles feel clearly that in spite of all that happened in past years they must now stand unconditionally by Prussia. They know that only the victory of the allied German and Austrian Empires will bring them the fulfillment of many wishes and hopes and that on the contrary the victory of Russia would be a catastrophe for them and their religion." Walter Kolarz, *Myths and Realities in Eastern Europe* (London, L. Drummond, 1946), p. 127. See also R. C. Foster to A. C. Coolidge, Apr. 7, 1919, *FR: Paris Peace Conference, 12*, 371.
37. Quoted by Henryk Frankel, *Poland*, p. 77.

Germany toward Poland. The German Government viewed with disfavor the prospect of a unified Poland; Austria-Hungary, on the other hand, hoped for this solution, in the belief that a Catholic Poland would be permanently bound to the Dual Monarchy. In order not to exacerbate German and Austrian differences, German General Headquarters, according to Hindenburg, intended to remain passive on the Polish question. When, however, the German governor of Warsaw convinced Hindenburg that an announcement of the creation of a Polish kingdom might result in a reinforcement of German armies by Polish troops, amounting to one million men, Hindenburg reconsidered his attitude, assuming that "a victorious Germany would be able in any case to settle the Polish question after the peace." [38] He delayed the decision to set up a Polish kingdom, which had been announced in the manifesto of the German and Austrian emperors, as long as he thought that there were possibilities of a separate peace with Russia. It was only when "these hopes of a separate peace with Russia broke down," he admitted, "that the manifesto was published in the early days of November, and that the recruiting of Polish volunteers, to which it referred, was entirely without result." [39] General Ludendorff gave similar reasons for the policy of the Central Powers. He mentioned that when he became quartermaster general he found an agreement which bound Germany and Austria-Hungary to establish an independent kingdom of Poland, a constitutional government, and a national army under a single command to be entrusted to Germany. This new Poland was to be accepted as a member of the alliance of the two empires, and its foreign policy was to be conducted accordingly. The two Central Powers mutually agreed upon their existing Polish possessions, and provided for frontier adjustments, at the expense of Russian Poland, which would have to be made for the greater security of their territory. The Polish claims, according to Ludendorff, were to be limited to strictly military necessities.[40]

The agreement which Ludendorff mentioned was probably the secret protocol signed in Vienna on August 12, 1916, between von Bethmann and Burian.[41] In this protocol the two governments agreed that Poland should be a hereditary and independent kingdom; that certain alterations of frontiers to the advantage of Ger-

---

38. Marshal von Hindenburg, *Out of My Life*, p. 222.
39. *Ibid.*, pp. 222-4.
40. Erich Ludendorff, *Ludendorff's Own Story* (New York, 1919), *2*, 441.
41. Ambassador in Germany [Gerard] to Secretary of State, Aug. 16, 1916, *FR: Lansing Papers, 1,* 694.

many were indispensable; that the district of Suwalki should not form part of the kingdom of Poland; that this kingdom should not have a foreign policy of its own; that the Polish Army should be commanded by the Germans; and that no territory forming part of Germany or Austria should be attached to the kingdom of Poland.[42]

Thus, driven by a desire for Polish manpower Germany and Austria ostentatiously proclaimed an "independent Polish Kingdom" on November 5, 1916, at Warsaw and at Lublin.[43] According to Dmowski this declaration rendered great service to the Polish cause. "It did more than anything else," he wrote, "to indicate to European statesmen the international importance of the Polish question. . . . It was a powerful incentive to occupy themselves seriously with the question."[44]

It cannot be denied that the pledge for the "resurrection" of the kingdom of Poland by the Central Powers was a highly significant event which did force the European powers to concern themselves seriously with the Polish question. In the Teutonic pledge there was a decided desire to confront the Allies at the peace conference with an accomplished fact, with a kingdom not *in posse* but *in esse*. If the Central Powers were to be the victors, as they expected to be, the creation of a kingdom of Poland, a strategic buffer state separating Russia from her allies, would not be a subject of bargaining. It would become, they believed, a part of the status quo at the end of the war and would serve as an immensely valuable bargaining point.

Were the Allies to win, and to insist in Russia's interest upon the dissolution of the new kingdom, they would then incur the blame of liberals throughout the world for destroying a nation and robbing a people of freedom. The Central Powers cleverly foresaw that the Allies would not be able to protest vigorously for fear the world might believe that the Allied plan for the rearrangement of Europe did not coincide with their already known protestations about principles of nationality and democracy.

Thus the Central Powers expected by the creation of the kingdom of Poland to sow discord in the ranks of the Allies at the end of the war. It was their belief that France and England were only

42. Smogorzewski, *Poland's Access to the Sea*, p. 84.
43. It was natural that in 1916 the German General Staff should turn to Poland as a possible source of new manpower. See Gerard to Secretary of State, Aug. 16, 1916, *FR: Lansing Papers, 1*, 694.
44. Dmowski, *Polityka Polska*, p. 282.

less afraid of Russia than of Germany. They counted upon the interests of France and England to oppose the westward march of a powerful Russia, in case of an Allied victory, and to uphold a German-dominated kingdom of Poland, which would also, should the Central Powers be defeated, provide them with a most necessary element of safety against Russia.

THE ALLIED POWERS AND THE POLISH QUESTION

Russian policy toward Poland developed on lines similar to that of Germany and Austria. On August 14, 1914, to counteract the German proclamation, Grand Duke Nicholas, as commander-in-chief of the Russian Army, issued a manifesto to the Poles, in which he said that "a century and a half ago, the living flesh of Poland had been torn to pieces, but her soul did not die. They [the Poles] lived by the hope that the hour would come when the Polish nation will be resurrected and will reconcile herself fraternally with Great Russia." [45]

This Saint Petersburg proclamation had a profound effect on the Poles within and outside Russian Poland. In answer to the Grand Duke's manifesto four political parties, under the leadership of the National Democratic party of Roman Dmowski, published the following declaration:

> The representatives of the undersigned political parties assembled on August 16th in Warsaw welcome the proclamation to the Poles of His Imperial Highness, the Supreme Commander of the Russian Armies, as an act of the greatest historical weight, and believe firmly that after the end of the war the promises expressed in the proclamation will be realized, and that the dreams of our fathers and forefathers will be fulfilled; that the body of Poland rent to pieces a century and a half ago, will be reunited and that the frontiers which have divided the Polish nation will vanish. The blood of her sons shed in common struggle against Germany will constitute equally a sacrifice offered on the altar of the resurrected fatherland. [46]

45. It continued: "The Russian Army brings the joyful tidings of this reconciliation. May the frontiers which have cut the Polish nation into pieces be effaced. May the Polish nation be reunited as one body *under the scepter of the Russian Emperor*. Under this scepter Poland will be reborn, free in her faith, her language and in self-government. . . ." Filasiewicz, *La Question polonaise*, p. 6, and Kumaniecki, *Odbudowa*, p. 27.

46. Frankel, *Poland*, p. 79. (The four political parties were: The National

In addition to the above declaration 69 representatives of Polish political parties and various social groups, including Roman Dmowski, W. Grabski, Prince Lubomirski, Count S. Lubienski, and Count M. Zamoyski, addressed a letter to Grand Duke Nicholas in which they welcomed "the sceptre of His Imperial Majesty" as loyal Russian subjects.[47]

This letter was soon implemented by the formation of a Polish legion which fought with the Russians against the Central Powers who, as we know, also had a Polish legion fighting with them. Within a few months Poles were fighting Poles for "Polish independence." "Look at my family!" said Count Joseph Potocki to Maurice Paléologue, "I am a Russian subject; my brother, Roman, is an Austrian subject; one of my brothers-in-law is a German subject, another one is an Austrian subject; all of my cousins and nephews, because of the circumstances of inheritance, are likewise divided among the three nations. In the bosom of the same race, we are condemned to kill each other!"[48]

The manifesto shows that the tsar decided to accord autonomous status to Poland. But why did he entrust the publication of the proclamation to the grand duke? Why did he not publish it himself as a direct act of his sovereign will? The moral effect would have certainly been more impressive and binding. But the Poles did not see the significance of this, nor did they question his motive. They greeted the manifesto with jubilation and deep emotion. When the declaration was given to Count Sigmund Wielopolski, president of the Polish group in the Council of the Empire, to translate into Polish, he exclaimed, "Que dans cette aurore s'allume le signe de la Croix, symbole des souffrances et de la résurrection des peuples!"[49]—and burst into tears. Count Joseph Potocki had it read in the churches and "cried like an infant."[50] Roman Dmowski, writing in 1925, stated that the proclamation was "beautifully written" and that it contained "the principal object for which Poles would fight with all their might."[51]

One of the first men to grasp the significance of the manifesto

Democratic party, the Polish Progressive party, the party of Realistic Action, and the Polish Progressive Union.)

47. *Ibid.*

48. Maurice Paléologue, *La Russie des tsars pendant la Grande Guerre* (Paris, Librairie Plon, 1921), *1, 169.*

49. *Ibid., 1, 82.*

50. *Ibid., 1, 168.*

51. Dmowski, *Polityka Polska,* p. 155.

was Paléologue. On August 13 he asked Sazonov why the tsar had not proclaimed it himself. Sazonov answered:

> That was my idea too at first. But Goremykin and Maklakov, who be it noted are hostile to the reconstruction of Poland, believed not without reason, that since the Poles of Galicia and Poznania are still under Austrian and Prussian domination, and since the conquest of the two provinces is but an expectation, a hope, the tsar cannot without risk of losing respect address himself in person to future subjects; whereas Grand Duke Nicholas, on the contrary, does not exceed his role of a Russian general in addressing himself to the Slav peoples whom he is going to free. . . . The tsar supports this opinion.[52]

Within two years the Russian Poles began to doubt the promises of the grand duke.[53] As soon as the Russian position improved on the eastern front the Russian Government began to evade its promises. Now it openly told the Poles that the manifesto signed by the grand duke was only a gesture of the military authority, not an act of the government, and that all previous promises were necessarily subordinate to the conquest of Prussian Poland. On August 14, 1916, having lost faith in Russia, the Polish National Committee for Cooperation with the Russian Government, formed after the grand duke's proclamation, moved to Switzerland in order "to concentrate all its hopes on France and England." [54] When Paléologue was informed of that move by Count Maurice Zamoyski, he said cynically: "L'autonomie sous le sceptre des Romanow ne leur suffit plus; il leur faut l'indépendance totale et absolue, la résurrection intégrale de l'État polonais, ils n'auront de cesse qu'ils n'aient fait triompher leur cause au Congrès de la paix." [55]

The attitude of Russia toward Poland remained unchanged until the Bolshevik Revolution of October 1917. The Provisional

---

52. Paléologue, *La Russie des tsars, 1*, 78–9.
53. *Ibid., 1*, 168. The Poles were able to gauge Russian policy toward Poland by the former's attitude to the German and Austrian proclamation of November 1916, which proclaimed autonomy of Russian Poland under the regime of an hereditary monarchy. The immediate reaction of the Russian press was that the tsar had lost his Polish crown: "La couronne de Pologne lui est arrachée de la tête." *Ibid., 3*, 77. Moreover, the proclamation of the Central Powers actually weakened the position of the Polish Russophiles.
54. *Ibid., 2*, 336.
55. *Ibid., 2*, 337.

Government established after the March revolution upheld the policy of the tsarist government toward Poland on March 29, 1917, but later changed to a declaration promising autonomy for Poland under Russian "guidance." In the April 1917 proclamation to the Poles the Lvov government announced that the Polish state, "united with Russia in a free military alliance, would form a bulwark against the Central Powers' drive toward the Slavonic peoples. The Russian Constituent Assembly would ultimately confirm the new 'brotherly union,' and would also give its consent to the territorial change in the Russian State." [56]

The ambiguity of policy of the Provisional Government did not dampen the enthusiasm of the pro-Russian Poles. They continued to support it until its fall. The Bolshevik Government which succeeded it declared in December 1917:

> . . . from the fact that the occupied territories belonged to the former Russian Empire the Russian Government draws no conclusion which would impose any constitutional obligation on the population of these regions in relation to the Russian Republic. . . . The new frontiers of the fraternal union of peoples of the Russian Republic and the peoples which desire to remain outside its borders must be defined by a free resolution of the peoples concerned.[57]

The Bolsheviks seem to have been the first of all the political groups among the belligerents to refer to the possibility of Poland's independence (and not only autonomy) as well as to the Polish people's right of self-determination. But we must remember that the Bolsheviks based this pro-Polish attitude on their hope that a Communist revolution might occur in Poland, which would bring her back into the Russian orbit and at the same time extend the revolution to the German border.[58]

The Polish National Committee for Cooperation with the Russian Government remained faithful to the Russian Imperial Government. They denounced the Bolshevik Revolution not because they doubted the Bolshevik pro-Polish attitude but because the Bolshevik ideology was repugnant to their conservative ideas and aristocratic background. When the Russians were obliged to re-

---

56. Filasiewicz, *La Question polonaise*, pp. 151, 153–5.

57. J. Bunyan and H. H. Fisher, *The Bolshevik Revolution 1917–1918* (Stanford, Calif., Stanford University Press, 1934), p. 494.

58. See below, pp. 35–7.

treat from Poland, the National Committee retreated too. Dmowski and his political associates appeared in Petrograd, in London, in Lausanne, in Paris, and finally in America. Soon after the Bolshevik Revolution they re-established the committee in Paris, to represent and speak for Poland. The composition of this committee was entirely consistent with the political views of its chairman Dmowski, and most of its members were National Democrats.[59]

The Western Powers supported the Russian solution of the Polish problem only so long as Russia remained their ally. Throughout they maintained a wise and honest reserve. For Russia, while still an ally, insisted that the Polish question was strictly a domestic issue and jealously guarded any attempt to put the future of Poland under the guarantee and control of the Allied Powers.[60] France and England were gratified to see that the Russian proclamation of August 1914 gave Poland assurance of autonomy. On the eve of that manifesto Paléologue assured the Russian Government that "the proclamation of Polish autonomy will be received in France not only as the first act of historical correction which will come out of the war but as an eminently sagacious act of considerable weight for the future which will *singularly facilitate the advance of the Russian armies in Poland.*" [61] Later when Sazonov told him of the background that led to the proclamation, Paléologue cited a sentence which P. Gratry uttered in 1863: "Depuis le partage de la Pologne, l'Europe est en état de péché mortel." [62]

France and Great Britain, not wishing to alienate Russia, did not interfere or try to influence Russia in her policy. As a matter of fact, in the first years of the war England was "not very enthusiastic over the idea of Polish independence." Her attitude toward Poland can be gauged from the conversation held by Colonel House with Lloyd George, Sir Edward Grey, and Arthur Balfour on February 14, 1916. It reveals that these British statesmen did not favor Polish independence. Balfour argued against Polish resurrection that if "Poland was made an independent kingdom, becoming a buffer-state between Russia and Germany, France would be at the mercy of Germany in the next war, for this reason, that

59. Anon., "America and Polish Politics," *New Republic, 17* (1918).
60. Sazonov to Izvolski, March 8, 1916. *FR: 1917*, Supplement 2, *1*, 501.
61. Paléologue, *La Russie des tsars, 2*, 308 (italics inserted).
62. *Ibid., 1*, 82.

Russia could not come to her aid without violating the neutrality of Poland." [63]

The Polish situation did not change when immediate exigencies of war compelled both Russia and Germany to issue proclamations in favor of an independent Poland. Germany meant by Poland only the Russian portion of Poland; Russia meant a Poland under her tutelage. Matters changed only with the Bolshevik Revolution and the entrance of the United States into the war in behalf of the policy announced by President Wilson. Of these two things the second was the more important, for while Russia's Provisional Government came out in favor of a free and united Poland, it nevertheless assumed that the new Poland would be in a "free military union" with Russia and that her boundaries were to be settled by the Russian Constituent Assembly.[64] Even the Bolshevik Revolution brought no promise for a future free, reunited, and independent Poland. It was only when the United States entered the conflict that Poland had for the first time a wholly disinterested force at work on her side, one whose commitment to self-determination for Poland had no strings or reservations.

THE BOLSHEVIKS AND THE POLISH QUESTION

Our next step on the path to world victory is the destruction of Poland.[65]

Trotsky

The Polish Socialist movement was one of the oldest in Central Europe. After the failure of the 1830 revolution Socialist groups were formed by the exiled emigrants in France and in Great Britain. No evidence is available as to the existence of organized Socialist parties in ethnographical Poland before 1880, when the Socialist Proletariat party, based on Marxist principles, was started. Not long after that the Proletariat concluded an alliance with the Russian Narodnaya Volya. Within a year of the establish-

63. Diary of Edward M. House, Feb. 20, 1916; MS in the House Collection of the Yale University Library. See also below, p. 73.

64. There is a translation of this proclamation, which reserved the right of a future Russian constituent assembly "to give its consent to the modification of Russian territory which will be indispensable for the formation of a free Poland," in Filasiewicz, *La Question polonaise*, p. 75.

65. Quoted by Winston S. Churchill, *The Aftermath* (New York, Scribners, 1929), p. 273.

ment of this alliance the Proletariat, because of its connections with Narodnaya Volya, was held responsible for the assassination of Tsar Alexander, suffered many arrests, and was finally liquidated.

Political heir of the Proletariat was the Socialist Democratic party of Poland and Lithuania (SDKPiL), founded in 1893.[66] This party, under the leadership of Rosa Luxemburg, considered that socialism was the primary aim to be achieved and that national freedom could be gained only if the governments of the occuping powers were overthrown by revolution. It stressed Socialist propaganda and international liberty within Poland. To the SDKPiL the cry "Long live Poland" signified, as it did to Marx, Engels, and Lenin, "Death to the Holy Alliance and Death to Autocratic Russia, Prussia, and Austria."

The outstanding figures in the 19th century who influenced the Polish Socialist movement and the later Bolshevik attitude toward Poland were Karl Marx and Friedrich Engels. Polish socialism received its Marxist traditions at first hand. Its leaders developed under the direct and personal influence of Marx and Engels who felt the Polish question to be highly important. It was perhaps because of the Marxian influence that Polish socialism maintained its independent character through its independent organizations, the Social Democratic party of Poland (SDKP) and the Polish Socialist party (*PPS*), in spite of the fact that Poland constituted part of the tsarist empire. This may also have been why, despite the intransigent internationalism of Rosa Luxemburg, the Lithuanian Social Democratic party, led by Tyszka and Jogiches, did not join the Russian Social Democratic party but entered the SDKP, forming the Social Democratic party of Poland and Lithuania (SDKPiL). Although the SDKPiL considered itself a part of the Russian Social Democratic party by virtue of its international principles, it submitted neither to the leadership of the latter nor to its program, always maintaining its own doctrine, which differed from that of the Bolsheviks.

Marx's and Engels' ostensible championship of the Polish cause was not based on the elaborate theory expounded in their famous *Manifesto of the Communist Party* of 1848. The fundamental

66. In December 1918, after the liberation of Poland, the SDKPiL and the left wing of the Polish Socialist party joined to form the Communist party of Poland.

reason for their enthusiasm for the Polish cause in 1848 lay in the fact that they saw, or thought they saw, in the Polish national movement a means by which the revolutionary cause might be advanced in Europe and at the same time a buffer state created that would separate the new, revolutionary Germany from the reactionary threat of tsarist Russia.[67] Marx and Engels wrote their appeals for Polish independence primarily as Germans and democrats who sought by revolutionary struggle to create a unified German nation and at the same time to destroy Russian autocracy. They continually demanded the reconstruction of the Polish state, because they considered the re-creation of an independent Poland necessary to the development of the revolution in Germany and to the attack upon the supporter of all European reaction—Russia. They assumed the outbreak of an agrarian revolution based upon the democratic peasant movement within Poland to be an essential condition of this restoration. "This reveals," Macdonald wrote, "the lack of understanding on the part of Marx and Engels in regard to the aristocratic nature of the Polish national movement." [68] In their view Poland was to become the tinder box which would ignite all Europe. Poland had to be restored to prepartition limits and given control of its great rivers as well as an extensive coastal strip along the Baltic. "The problem here is not one of restoration of a shadow and ghost like Poland, but the erection of a state with a sufficient and adequate foundation. Poland must have nothing less than the territorial limits of 1772; it must have not only territory, but likewise the mouths of its great streams, and in addition an adequate coastal strip on the Baltic." [69]

Soon after the revolution of 1848 Marx wrote in the *Neue Rheinische Zeitung:*

As long as we help to oppress the Poles and as long as we bind a part of Poland to Germany so long are we bound to Russia and Russian policy, and will be unable to break fundamentally with patriarchal feudal absolutism here at home. . . .

The creation of a democratic Poland is the first condition for the establishment of a democratic Germany. . . . And it is not merely a matter of building a Poland that is independent

67. H. Malcolm Macdonald, "Marx, Engels and the Polish National Movement," *Journal of Modern History, 13* (1941), 321–34.
68. *Ibid., 13,* 322.
69. *Neue Rheinische Zeitung,* Aug. 19, 1848. Quoted by Macdonald, *op. cit.,* p. 326.

only on paper, but building a state on a lasting foundation capable of genuine existence. Poland must regain at least the territory that was hers in 1772.[70]

From the reference to 1772 we see that Marx wanted to restore Poland to her prepartition boundaries which, at the time of his writing, were inhabited by Czechs, Slovaks, Slovenes, Ukranians, Lithuanians, and other Slavic peoples. His proposal suggests that Marx had no intention of championing the cause of these peoples. He believed that the Slav peoples lacked historical consciousness and were too variegated to unite and too weak, both culturally and politically, to live as separate nations. According to Bertram Wolfe, Marx held the nationalist movements of these Slavic peoples "mere powerless fantasies of utopian intellectuals," and·believed that if they were given independence "they would become inevitable puppets or prey of the steadily expanding Russian State, a State which menaced all democratic movements in Western Europe and which therefore must not be permitted to expand." [71] Marx and Engels, we must remember, ventured these conclusions as a result of the ostensible Polish nationalism which expressed itself in the revolution of 1848.

"The animus of Marx and Engels toward Russian and Slav peoples," Bertram Wolfe wrote, "came from their experiences of the year 1848. They refined and modified, but never fully re-examined those conclusions during the rest of their lives. . . ." [72] In 1848 Vienna, Berlin, Warsaw, Paris, and some Italian cities rose in revolt, but Russian troops and the loyal Slavs of Austria helped to restore the Hapsburgs to their capital and throne. It was for this reason, Wolfe contended, that Marx and Engels became convinced no revolution could triumph in Western Europe so long as Russia remained a great power; and for this reason they began to urge war on Russia. They wrote:

> Only war with Russia is a war for revolutionary Germany, a war in which it can wash away its sins of the past, can get courage [*sich ermannen*], can defeat its own autocrats, and in which, as beseems a people shaking off the chains of a long passive slavery, can purchase the propaganda of civilization with

70. Bertram D. Wolfe, *Three Who Made a Revolution* (New York, Dial Press, 1948), p. 574.
71. *Ibid.*, p. 571.
72. *Ibid.*

the sacrifice of its own sons, making itself free within while it is freeing itself without . . .[73]

Within a few years after 1848 Engels changed his attitude toward Poland. He still believed that the act of creating a free Poland would facilitate the creation of a German republic but he no longer believed that Poland could exist as a free nation.

Marx and Engels sought to make a revolutionary Poland the foundation on which a German revolution might be built. But in time Prussian domination was once more firmly established over Poland, and the agrarian revolution they had so confidently expected did not take place. Consequently they modified their views. Since they had not basically supported the Polish revolution as a "national movement," they ceased to advocate Polish independence as soon as the probability of a successful social and economic revolution in that country seemed unlikely of realization. As a result Engels began to deny Poland any right to a "national" existence. This abandonment of Poland is well demonstrated in a letter of Engels to Marx:

> The more I think over the business the clearer it becomes to me that the Poles as a nation are done for and can only be made use of as an instrument until Russia herself is swept into the agrarian revolution. From that moment onwards Poland will have absolutely no more reason for existence. The Poles have never done anything in history except play at brave, quarrelsome stupidity. Any one cannot point to a single instance in which Poland represented progress successfully, even if only in relation to Russia, or did anything at all of historic importance. . . .[74]

Engels no longer believed that a strong feeling of nationalism existed among the Polish people. Nor did he have any hopes of an indigenous uprising in Poland.[75]

Yet the pair still regarded Poland as the barrier separating Germany from the "barbaric despotism" of Russia—a barrier which they held to be necessary for the free development of capitalism in Germany.[76]

73. *Ibid.*, pp. 572–3.
74. Karl Marx to Friedrich Engels, May 23, 1851, *Selected Correspondence*, pp. 37–8.
75. *Ibid.*
76. *Ibid.*, pp. 144–6.

Marx's hope for a revolution in Germany was shattered by the growing power of Bismarck. The latter's unification of Germany called for different tactics and approaches to the problem of destroying European despotism. Until then Marx had hoped that an independent Poland would destroy Prussian autocracy in Germany; now this possibility had vanished. Yet Marx was not apt to give up an idea which he had expounded for more than twenty years. If an independent Poland could no longer destroy Prussian despotism, it could still put an end to Russian autocracy! Soon after Bismarck's rise to power Marx began to counsel his Russian admirers to champion Polish independence as a means of destroying the Russian Empire.[77]

Marx died in 1883, and Engels twelve years later. Nationalism, in the absence of the proletarian revolutions which they had expected, took possession of increasing numbers of people. After 1905 it became a grave problem for the Socialist movement. There was a need, therefore, for some of Marx's and Engels' many disciples to select from the masters' utterances guide lines for attitudes toward the new nationalism. Among the prominent Marxists, who addressed themselves to this problem was Lenin.

Only after 1912 did Lenin develop a complete program on the Polish problem. When in that year he moved to the Polish-Austrian city of Cracow, he became aware of the Polish national question, now intensified by division, disputes, plots, and controversies. In this Polish city he had to take account of the nationalism of Pilsudski's Polish Socialist party and the antinationalism of Rosa Luxemburg's Polish and Lithuanian Social Democratic party. Moreover, living in Austria, he was soon struck by the Austrian Poles' hatred of Russia.

Animosity toward Russia, Lenin believed, made the Poles class conscious. He was willing, therefore, to support Polish aspirations, believing that as soon as their class consciousness and hatred of Russia disappeared their nationalism would die away. In order to further this end he was even willing to allow Poland to separate from Russia.[78] In 1913, when no possibilities for separation existed yet either for Poland or for other nations, Lenin could freely

77. *Ibid.*, p. 287.

78. In 1941 Stalin told Sikorski that Lenin had said: "The Poles hate Russia and not without reason. We cannot ignore the strength of their national feeling. Our revolution will have to treat them very gently and even allow them to break away from the Russian Empire if need be." See Isaac Deutscher, *Stalin* (New York and London, Oxford University Press, 1949), p. 116.

grant these countries national status. He had nothing to lose; what he had to gain was party unity, his real concern in 1913. He preached separation but expected the independent nations, once they came into existence, to unite again.

Careful study of Lenin's speeches which deal with the Polish question shows that he based his appeal for separation on two important assumptions. He hoped, first of all, that those nations that wished to separate before 1917 would join the Soviet state after the seizure of power in Russia. In order to facilitate this eventual fusion it was necessary, he believed, for the Bolsheviks to emphasize the right of the Poles to separate, but at the same time to convince the Poles that they themselves should emphasize the right to unite. His second assumption was that until the Bolsheviks had attained power in Russia they must champion the right of separation for strategic reasons, but once they seized power they should do their utmost to bring in all the neighboring nation-states. In his speech on the national question on May 12, 1917, Lenin said:

> If Finland, if Poland, if the Ukraine break away from Russia, it is nothing terrible. Wherein is it bad? One who says so, is a chauvinist. One must be insane to continue the policy of Tsar Nicholas. Norway has separated from Sweden. . . . Are we to continue this policy of the Tsars? This is a repudiation of internationalist tactics, this is chauvinism of the worst brand. . . . *In both peoples among the proletariat of Norway and Sweden mutual confidence increased after separation.*[79]

In the same speech he expressed quite clearly his hope that after separation the "separated" states would join Bolshevized Russia. He continued: "Only when this ideal [right of separation] is realised, will faith in Russian democracy be strengthened, will the Finns refuse to separate." [80]

Here also he appealed to the Marxist section in Poland to work for the separation of Poland, but he made it clear they should see to it that the Poles desired a closer union with the new Russia: "We Russians must emphasise the right to separate, while the Poles must emphasise the right to unite. . . . In Russia we must stress the right of separation for the subject nations, while in Poland we must stress the right of such nations to unite." [81]

79. Vladimir I. Lenin, *Collected Works* (New York, International Publishers, 1929), *20*, Bk. 1 (*The Revolution of 1917*), 313 (italics inserted).
80. *Ibid.*
81. *Ibid.*, p. 312.

That Lenin's championship of Polish independence was based on strategic considerations can be seen from the following quotation of his speech:

> Instead of teaching the Polish workers that chauvinists have no place in the Socialist Party and that only those Social-Democrats are real democrats who maintain that the Polish people ought to be free, the Polish Social-Democrats argue that because they find the union with the Russian workers advantageous they are opposed to Poland's separation. They have a perfect right to do so. But these people fail to understand that to enhance internationalism it is not at all necessary to reiterate the same words. . . .
>
> The method of accomplishing a Socialist revolution under the slogan: "Down with the boundaries" is an utter absurdity. . . .
>
> But if the Soviet seizes power tomorrow, that will no longer constitute a "method of Socialist Revolution," and we shall then say: Germany, out with your armies from Poland. . . .
>
> When the Socialist Revolution has become a reality, and not a method, then we shall say: Comrades, come unto us . . . and the slogan "Down with the boundaries" will be a true slogan. . . .[82]

Lenin, it is evident, distinguished between the "method of Socialist Revolution" and the "reality" of the revolution. By this he meant that in order to bring about the revolution in Russia it was necessary for the long-term aims of bolshevism temporarily to give way to immediate goals. Lenin was a realist who saw in the separation of Poland a means of facilitating the immediate seizure of power. But after this had been achieved an independent Poland, as Engels had said, would have "no more reason for existence." It was Lenin's hope that his revolution would spread over Europe like wildfire and bring neighboring states into the new international order. Poland would then constitute a bridge for the spread of the revolution into Europe. The Bolsheviks, who were fully acquainted with the intolerance of the Poles and their political and religious chauvinism, were doubtless inspired with the idea that a few years of Polish self-rule would create a strong anti-Polish *irredenta*, which the Bolsheviks, with their consummate talent for fishing in troubled waters, would be able to use against the Poles.

82. *Ibid.*, p. 313.

Accordingly, at the outset of 1918, the Bolsheviks abjured all claims to conquer the Polish nation, save by ideas and extensive propaganda.[83] But when, with the help of the American and Western Allies who were afraid of the spread of bolshevism, a Polish Republic was established, it became, from the moment of its inception, hostile to the Soviet Government. This hostility finally resulted in a Polish-Russian war. In the autumn of 1919 the Poles, taking advantage of the civil war in Russia, seized Vilna in defiance of its award to Lithuania by the League of Nations, and occupied Minsk and a considerable portion of Volhynia and Podolia. In the face of General Denikin's successes against the Red Army, however, they froze into inactivity.[84] Paderewski was afraid of a powerful military Russia developing under Kolchak.[85] On the other hand Pilsudski feared that the success of the White Armies, which were pledged to restore the territorial possessions of the tsarist empire, would prove inimical to Poland. As soon as the Red Army began to win, the Polish Army sprang into activity again. By April 1920 the Poles took Kiev. But their victory was short-lived. They had to evacuate the city and were hotly pursued by Tukhachevsky's army in the north and Yegorov's and Budienny's armies in the south. The Soviet Government sought not only to repulse the attack but to carry the Bolshevik Revolution itself into Poland and thus force open a door for communism into all Europe.

Lenin urged an all-out offensive against Poland. The slogan "Down with the boundaries" was now a "reality." He hoped that the entry of the Red Army into Poland would spur the Polish working class to a Communist revolution. Yet his main interest was not Poland but Germany, which at that time was undergoing revolutionary ferment. The Polish-Russian war gave him the opportunity to expand communism to Western Europe. "By attacking Poland," he wrote, "we are attacking the Allies; by destroying the Polish Army, we are destroying the Versailles Treaty upon which rests the whole system of present international relationship. . . . Had Poland become sovietized . . . the Versailles Treaty would have been terminated and the system built on victory over Germany would have been likewise destroyed."[86]

Within a few weeks Soviet forces approached Warsaw. The

83. W. F. Reddaway, "The Peace Conference," in Reddaway, *Cambridge History of Poland*, p. 490. See also *FR: Paris Peace Conference, 1919, 2*, 414.
84. *FR: Paris Peace Conference, 1919, 9*, 784.
85. *FR: Russia, 1919*, p. 342.
86. Lenin, *Collected Works, 17*, 334.

Bolshevik army was tired, weakened by many losses, and its lines of communication were dangerously stretched. As a result Pilsudski, with the help of the French General Weygand, was able to destroy the enemy and eventually drive the Red Army out of Poland. After this defeat Lenin seldom spoke of Poland. Only after the Red forces were defeated in their attempt to make a Soviet republic of Poland did the Soviet Government fully recognize the right of Poland to become an independent state.[87]

87. It remained for Stalin to avenge the Soviet defeat. The bitterness that rankled in the hearts of the Soviet leaders was permitted full expression in connection with the Russo-German Nonaggression Pact of 1939. The official Soviet press announcement that "Poland had ceased to exist," coupled with Molotov's famous phrase, "One swift blow to Poland by the German Army and then by the Red Army and nothing remained of this ugly offspring of the Versailles Treaty," indicates the depth of emotion that had been tapped by the event itself. See V. Molotov, *Report to the Fifth Session of the Supreme Soviet,* Oct. 31, 1939.

3. The Poles in American History and Tradition

THE ENTRANCE of the United States into the war was the final, fortuitous factor that made Polish independence a reality. With the involvement of America in the affairs of Europe came the triumph of the principle that every nation must be free and that such freedom is the essential condition of a lasting peace.

Five important factors have influenced America's friendship toward Poland. These were the pro-Polish tradition which had grown out of America's gratitude toward Thaddeus Kosciuszko and Casimir Pulaski, Poles who fought for American independence during the Revolutonary War; the sympathy which Americans have always felt for oppressed peoples; the world economic situation, and particularly conditions in Poland during the first World War that brought about the formation in the United States of Polish relief organizations; most importantly, the use of political pressure by Polish-Americans during the war; and lastly President Wilson's ambition to transform Europe according to his political philosophy. Another factor worked negatively: since the Polish nation had not existed throughout most of the United States' history, no friction had arisen to impair the friendship of the two peoples.

What are the history and tradition of the Poles in America? According to an entertaining legend popular during the first World War, the Poles began to come to America sixteen years before Columbus discovered the continent; a Pole, John of Kolno, reputedly commanded Danish ships which touched the coast of Labrador in 1476.[1] In spite of this tale there are no indications of Polish settlements of any size in America before the War of Independence.

The traditional attachment of America for Poland began during the Revolution, when Kosciuszko and Pulaski gave distinguished service to the American cause. Both came to America upon Franklin's recommendations to fight in the Revolutionary Army. Count Casimir Pulaski joined the American forces as a volunteer and ended up in command of a mixed body of light infantry and cavalry armed with lances. These troops, known as Pulaski's Le-

1. H. H. Fisher and Sidney Brooks, *America and the New Poland* (New York, Macmillan, 1928), p. 50.

gion, performed valuable service in southern campaigns. Pulaski was mortally wounded in the defense of Savannah and died on board the U.S. brig *Wasp*, to which he had been taken for medical treatment.

Kosciuszko's career in America left an enduring tradition. He was both the military associate and personal friend of Washington. His liberal ideas won him the lifelong friendship of Jefferson. At first Kosciuszko served as an aide on Washington's staff, later he was appointed colonel of engineers and sent to the northern army. There he organized the defense of Ticonderoga, Mount Independence, and West Point, and contributed to the decisive victory over Burgoyne by his construction of the defenses at Bemis Heights. His distinguished service won him promotion to the rank of brigadier general, and at the end of the war he received the thanks of Congress with the rank of major general. He returned to Poland in 1789, and in 1794 started an unsuccessful revolution against Russia which led to the third and final partition of Poland. The loss of Polish independence and Kosciuszko's subsequent captivity in Russia aroused American sympathy and strengthened the already existing affection between the people of America and Poland. To Venceslas de Tworkowski the friendship between Washington and Kosciuszko was stronger than historical alliances. "Leur parente," he wrote in 1919, "était spirituelle." [2]

It was not until 1832 that the first thin stream of Polish emigration to the United States began. But it increased in volume in the 1840's as a result of European revolutions. By 1860 there were Poles in every state and territory of the Union except Dakota. During the American Civil War Poles were to be found in the Confederate as well as in the Union armies, depending upon their state residence. The largest numbers settled in New York, Texas, California, and Wisconsin.

The Polish revolution of 1863 neither increased Polish emigration to the United States nor influenced public opinion. When Napoleon III invited the United States to join in a protest against Russian policy in Poland, the United States Government declined on the ground that it was contrary to American policy to intervene in purely European affairs. This attitude can perhaps be explained by the fact that the American people were at that time too involved in the Civil War to pay much attention to Poland, and the

2. Abbé Venceslas de Tworkowski, *Wilson et la question polonaise* (Saint-Moritz, St. Augustin, 1919), p. 11.

government could not afford to antagonize Russia, which was then believed to be friendly to the North.

Although the number of Polish immigrants remained small until the 1880's, a few agricultural colonists came with their families before that time. Among them were the groups that founded Panna Maria in Texas during the 1850's, Polonia in Wisconsin in the same decade, and Parisville, Michigan.[3]

As the number kept increasing, male immigration and scattered settlements became characteristic.[4] The trend toward the cities began in the seventies and eighties. Before long Poles began to draw together in "nucleated centers," occasionally forming a "boarding-house complex." [5] These centers gradually formed in each city a Polish colony known as *Polonia*.[6] Engaging in unskilled manual labor and knowing little of the language and customs of America, the immigrant was naturally drawn toward others of his own kind. Although he endured some of the discrimination shown against all foreign groups, he found freedom in relative absence of pressure for assimilation and he soon began to organize his compatriots with great fervor. The United States Government made no effort, as did the German and Russian governments, to denationalize the Poles. Nevertheless the first Polish immigrants thought of themselves as exiles from the Old World rather than as immigrants in the New.[7]

After 1871, as a result of Bismarck's anti-Polish and anti-Catholic policy, Polish emigration from German Poland increased considerably. But from 1880 on economic rather than political or religious reasons provided the motive for Polish emigration to the United States. As soon as Germany became an industrial state, she began to absorb Poles in her rapidly expanding industries; emigration from provinces controlled by Germany decreased, while that from Russian-controlled Poland and Galicia increased.[8] This shift had a great effect on the type of Polish immigrants to the United States. The Poles from Russian Poland and Galicia were

3. Emily G. Balch, *Our Slavic Fellow Citizens* (New York, 1910), pp. 228–30.

4. *Ibid.,* pp. 135–7.

5. Thomas and Znaniecki, *The Polish Peasant, 2,* 1512–24.

6. *Ibid.*

7. Karol Wachtl, *Polonja w Ameryce* (Philadelphia, Polish Star Publishing Co., 1944), p. 85. For a long time Polish immigrants did not even strive to obtain American citizenship. It was only during the first World War that Polish-American leaders, aware of the importance and power of votes, began to use pressure to force their brethren to apply for American citizenship.

8. Paul Fox, *The Poles in America* (New York, 1922), pp. 58–9.

mostly illiterate peasants, politically inexperienced and fanatically religious. They came to America because agriculture in their respective regions was backward and peasant land was insufficient to support the increasing population. Galicia had no industry to absorb surplus hands, and emigration from that region grew enormously. It was only in the last few years of the 19th century that industry in Russian Poland expanded notably and was able to absorb at least a part of the swelling population. But the economic crisis of 1901–1903, prolonged to 1908 by the revolutionary disturbance of 1905, accelerated emigration during those years.

The early 20th-century Polish immigrants were welcomed in America. American industry hungered for men. Polish peasants and other immigrants from Eastern Europe answered its need by working in the mines and factories of Pennsylvania and in the Middle West. The nature of urban life and of their employment made the problem of social readjustment difficult. Polish immigrant colonies, rural and urban, found themselves surrounded by other peoples of different languages and customs, which intensified the consciousness of their nationality.

As immigration increased the Polonias in America flourished proportionally. The Polonia was organized in two chronological stages. The preliminary period of transition and orientation gradually gave way to the forming of mutual benefit organizations or "societies." The wealthy members of the community were often the leaders of the new group. In time the society became a sort of social club that arranged dances, musicals, dramatic entertainment, and lectures in which the Polish language and Polish customs were always used. Other nationalities gradually moved out and left homes or tenements vacant, which were soon appropriated by more incoming Poles.[9]

The second step of the colony was to organize the Polish parish. Like other nationality groups predominantly Catholic, the Poles on their arrival in America found themselves attending churches in which their own language was not heard. The colony soon began to press for Polish prayers and Polish priests. The Polish peasants, while retaining a good deal of superstition and magic in their religion, kept it subordinate to the power of the priest, who was obeyed implicitly.[10] Lacking in political training, the Polish people regarded the priest as the only leader they could

9. Thomas and Znaniecki, *The Polish Peasant, 2,* 1545–47.
10. *Ibid., 1,* 285. See also Sula Benet, *Song, Dance and Custom,* pp. 36–8.

trust; they brought this attitude with them to their adopted land. At first the Roman Catholic parish priests were mostly concerned with the social, cultural, and material interests of the immigrants. For a long time they restricted the assimilation of the Polish immigrants into the American surroundings. "That we in America are Poles," Karol Wachtl recorded, "that there exists a Polish-American community, is all due to our religion and the contribution of the Roman Catholic Church—the Faith of our Fathers." [11] The large Polish-American community which had grown out of the mass immigration of peasant labor since the seventies long retained its manners, religion, and even language with the stubbornness of peasant nature. "The Polish Roman Catholic parish," Roman Dyboski wrote, "became the Polish immigrant worker's chief center of social organization, and schools and colleges, when they developed among the immigrant community, were largely conducted by nuns and priests. Purely secular organizations, when they arose, originally served the purpose of social insurance. . . ." [12] According to Wachtl, the parish was the first "organizational cell" which transplanted Polish ways of life to the shores of America. "Without the Church," he added, "we would have lost our identity." [13]

With the establishment of the parish, center of all social and cultural activities, the tendency to congregate grew stronger. New institutions sprang up, the most important of which was the parochial school, usually built soon after the church. The parochial schools allowed a disproportionate amount of time for learning the catechism, less time for reading, writing, arithmetic and geography. Parents frequently took the position that children grew away from them and from the stabilizing influence of Polish customs too rapidly when they entered public schools. Desiring some means of cushioning the sudden cultural shock to the younger generation, parents and priest saw to it that the Polish language was taught as well as something of the history and culture of Poland. As a result many children who spent six or seven years in a parochial school could scarcely pass an examination for the fifth grade in a public elementary school.[14] When the anticlerical Polish newspaper, the *Kuryer Polski,* began stirring up this issue between 1910 and 1912 with the proposal that the Polish language be

11. Wachtl, *Polonja,* p. 78.
12. Roman Dyboski, *Poland in World Civilization* (New York, J. M. Barrett, 1950), p. 114.
13. Wachtl, *Polonja,* p. 77.
14. Balch, *Our Slavic Fellow Citizens,* Appendix 26, pp. 477–8.

taught in the public schools of Milwaukee along with German, Catholic leaders regarded the step as a program to destroy the parochial school system and bitterly resisted it. Neither side would yield. In 1912 Archbishop Messmer of the Milwaukee archdiocese issued a decree forbidding all Catholics to read the *Kuryer Polski;* the newspaper rejoined with a damage suit for $100,000, which was thrown out by the courts.[15] Since then the Polish parochial system has not been successfully challenged.

Before long the purely local character of the Polonia no longer sufficed, and the demand to gather all Polish-Americans in a common body began in the latter part of the 19th century. From the first the strongest of these organizations was the Polish National Alliance (Zwiazek Narodowy Polski), which in 1880 united the efforts of local fraternal orders or societies by giving them a rallying point. Its purposes as originally stated were to lay the foundation for an institution that would work for the material and moral amelioration fund, protect the Polish immigrants, prepare them for American citizenship, and commemorate Polish historic events.

The Polish National Alliance was organized as a secular and nonsectarian group with no religious qualifications for membership. In addition to its stated aims it promoted a patriotic national Polish spirit and gave the immigrant a fuller knowledge of Polish culture and history.[16] The organization also furthered the idea that the Poles in America were a strong and integral part of the old Polish nation. In the free America the Alliance took the immigrant, often without a well-developed Polish national spirit, and helped to create in him a new patriotic consciousness. The process was tremendously aided by both the Polish clergy and publications in the United States.

The Alliance was led by the intellectual elite who enjoyed considerable prestige and respect among the Poles in the homeland for their service in keeping Polish culture alive. In America they continued the same function. The Alliance had a superior press, and even founded a college of its own in 1912, Alliance College, at Cambridge Springs, Pennsylvania.[17] Its chief newspapers were the Polish *Daily Zgoda* and the weekly *Zgoda* (*Harmony*) which were distributed to all its members throughout the country.[18]

15. Edmund A. Olszyk, *The Polish Press in America* (Masters thesis, Marquette University Press, Milwaukee, 1940), pp. 25–6.
16. Thomas and Znaniecki, *The Polish Peasant, 2,* 1594–1602.
17. *Ibid.*
18. Olszyk, *Polish Press,* p. 17.

Although an overwhelming majority of the members of the Alliance were Catholic, many clerical leaders were dissatisfied with an organization that did not stress religion. In 1873 an informal federation of parish leaders joined their efforts to promote religious unity among the Poles. They called themselves the Polish Roman Catholic Union of America (Zjednoczenie Polskie Rzymsko-Katolickie w Ameryce). At first this union failed to thrive and became inactive. A few months after the Polish National Alliance was founded, the Reverend Vincent Barzynski with several other priests revived the Union in order to balance the secular influence of the Alliance.[19] Its purpose was not purely negative; its positive aims were to preserve the integrity of Polish parishes from absorption by the Catholic Church hierarchy in America, and to resist "Americanization" of church members.[20]

While not emphasizing patriotic motives in quite the same way as the Polish National Alliance, the Polish Roman Catholic Union nevertheless had many aims that tended to overlap those of the rival organization. The most important was that of preserving Polish national culture in the United States.[21] For a time considerable strife and bitterness flourished between the two organizations. The Polish-American who wanted to become identified with one or the other was often caught in a dilemma. If he joined the Union the members of the Alliance would say that he was not a true patriot; if he joined the Alliance the Union would accuse him of being untrue to his religion. The Reverend Waclaw Kruszka describes the bitter factionalism of these two groups in this manner: "For some time neither Catholics nor Poles existed in America, but only Unionists (P.R.C.U.) or Alliancists (P.N.A.); who was not a member of the Alliance, him the P.N.A. did not regard as a Pole; while whoever was not a member of the P.R.C.U., the P.R.C.U. did not regard as a Catholic." [22]

19. Thomas and Znaniecki, *The Polish Peasant*, *2*, 1604.
20. *Ibid.*, *2*, 1604–05. See also Wachtl, *Polonja*, p. 164.
21. The reason for this policy of the Polish clergy is perhaps best explained by Ralph Butler: "In case of the Poles . . . nationalism has been identified with the Church. In fact, religion and nationality in Poland are so thoroughly identified that the Poles have always endeavored to identify 'Pole,' 'Latin' and 'Catholic,' so that a Russian who was not a Greek, but a Latin Catholic would frequently call himself a Pole. The Polish priests encouraged him to do so." Ralph Butler, *The New Eastern Europe* (New York, Longmans, Green and Co., 1919), p. 65.
22. Waclaw Kruszka, *Historja Polska w Ameryce* (Milwaukee, Wis. Spolka Wydawniczej Kuryera 1905), *4*, 32. The lesser Polish organizations were the Polish Women's Alliance, Polish Falcons' Alliance, Polish Alma Mater, Polish Union of America, Polish National Council, Polish Uniformed Societies, Polish Central Relief Committee, and St. Joseph's Polish Union.

The Polish press in America played an important role in shaping the attitudes of Polish-Americans. Here many immigrants learned to read their mother tongue and acquired the habit of reading newspapers. Olszyk listed the purposes of the Polish press as first, to keep alive unity and understanding among Polish immigrants; second, to inform them of the advantages of American citizenship; and third, after the first World War, to bring news of fellow Poles and their activities in Poland and throughout the world.[23]

The Polish newspapers in America lacked distinction and represented divergent points of view. Many of them were conducted by the priests for purposes of edification, some were anticlerical, others were political; of the latter, part favored labor and Socialist causes, and a substantial number found *raison d'être* and support as organs of the many Polish associations.[24] The mortality rate was high: between 1870 and 1900, 150 began publication; by 1905 only 49 survived.[25]

The influential Polish *Daily Zgoda*, organ of the Polish National Alliance, was strongly against Americanization. Even after the first World War, when this newspaper was forced, because of the steadily increasing number of readers who could understand English, to publish English columns, it pursued an ingenious policy of anti-Americanization. In the Polish editorials it denounced acculturation, whereas in the English editorials it lauded the American way of life.[26]

23. Olszyk, *Polish Press,* p. 13.
24. Balch, *Our Slavic Fellow Citizens,* pp. 383–4.
25. Olszyk, *Polish Press,* p. 43.
26. See Appendix.

4. American Poles and the Polish Question

BEFORE THE FIRST World War the Polish-American press, Polish Catholic organizations, and the various secular Polish societies were primarily concerned with the social, cultural, and material interests of the immigrants. Their activities were mainly focused on local issues. The outbreak of the war, however, caused the national issue of Poland and America to overshadow local problems. Polish-American leaders, lay and ecclesiastical, began to concern themselves with the large question of Polish nationalism in Europe and to encourage the Poles in America to participate in the struggle for Polish independence. But the Polish-Americans, now made more aware by Polish agitators than ever before of their "hyphenated" state, did not unite into a single political bloc. As the war continued, differences among them increased.

The Polish immigrants to this country in a great majority of instances had come for economic rather than for political reasons: they considered their residence in America as permanent, not temporary. Most of them were illiterate peasants with no political experience. America was to them an economic and religious haven, far away from Poland and outside of, and little concerned with, European political questions. When the war brought hope for the re-establishment of a Polish nation, Polish political leaders, indigenous and foreign, began to exert political and social pressure in an attempt to unite them into a strong political bloc to influence American foreign policy. Influential Poles from Russia, Austria, and Germany came to America to remind them that they were the "fourth part of Poland" and tried to enlist their aid for the particular country they represented. Ignace Jan Paderewski, famous pianist turned politician and orator, told them that "the Poles in America do not need any Americanization." [1] He found powerful support in the Catholic clergy who were a potent source of resistance to Americanization and assimilation.[2] The speeches

1. Anon., "The Spirit of Poles in America," *Survey, 40* (1918), 721.
2. The Polish nationalists found powerful support in the Catholic clergy. "In their churches," wrote A. Kaupas, "the Polish immigrants feel at home. The Church is a little corner of the distant fatherland. It is thus in America that religion has become the most powerful source of resistance against Americanization (assimilation)." Quoted by Robert E. Park, *The Immigrant Press and Its Control* (New York and London, Harper, 1922), p. 53.

of these orators were supplemented by a flood of books, pamphlets, and posters glorifying and exaggerating the Poles' participation in American affairs. Usually they hinted that the Poles in America had a right to demand help from the American Government. One widely used poster bore the legend: "Kosciuszko and Pulaski fought for American freedom. Will you help America fight for freedom in Poland?" [3] For the first time, during the war years, the Poles in America became conscious of their contribution to the United States.

Past entanglements, divisions, and intrigues in Poland had left their impress upon the Poles not only at home but also in America. The fact that Austria-Hungary had treated them better than had either Russia or Germany created a relatively large pro-Austrian group among them.[4] With these mixed sympathies, the American Poles became divided by misunderstanding, and they lacked a concrete and definite program. "One section was pro-German, one pro-Austrian, under the delusion that the Central Empires would finally win." [5] These discords, which were carried over to American soil from European conditions, were further intensified by a struggle between the clericals and anticlericals for supremacy in American-Polish organizations and affairs and by the campaign of misrepresentation carried on by the majority factions (pro-Allied Powers) against the minority parties (pro-Central Powers and those thoroughly Americanized Poles who were loyal to the American policy of neutrality). "The [Polish] immigrants," Park wrote, "frequently carried their political differences into their support of the home country, and seemed to be fighting one another as hard as, or harder than, they resisted the enemy." [6] The effect of this campaign of misrepresentation, at once personal and partisan,[7] was threefold: (a) it created discord and intensified strife; (b) by discrediting a number of men of great vigor, intelligence, and learning it closed important channels of communication and information to the American public and even to the

3. G. I. Ralton, "The United States and the Polish Question in World War I," *Polish Review, 6* (1946), 6.

4. Some Polish-American newspapers were even subsidized by the Austro-Hungarian Empire. See Park, *Immigrant Press,* p. 433.

5. Edward M. House, "Paderewski: The Paradox of Europe," *Harper's Magazine, 152* (1925), 30.

6. Park, *Immigrant Press,* p. 202.

7. See Dewey to Wilson, Sept. 25, 1918, Private papers of Woodrow Wilson, in the Woodrow Wilson Collection, Library of Congress. The partisan division, unusually acute and large scale, was complicated by the struggle of individuals for power.

United States Government; (c) it deprived the government of a large part of the active aid which the leaders of the Polish minority groups were capable of giving with the Liberty Loans, Red Cross drives, and particularly, when the United States entered the war, in allaying industrial unrest and speeding up factory, mining, and ship work connected with the war.[8] Yet the campaign of the clericals and followers of Roman Dmowski to capture the voice of the Polish-Americans did not succeed until the end of 1918.[9] The man who "united" the Poles in America in favor of the rebirth of Poland was Ignace Jan Paderewski.

Paderewski came to the United States late in 1915 as the "representative" of the pro-Russian Polish National Committee that Roman Dmowski headed.[10] His specific instructions were to make the Allies, as they led the world out of war into victory and peace, conscious of the "historical crime of 1795." [11] It was his duty to educate public opinion so that people would back those political leaders who would be sympathetic to Poland when the time for readjustment came. All the representatives of the Polish National Committee were told that "the name of Poland, forgotten for so long in the political world, must sound again from chancelleries and from editorial offices; the world must be conscious of a brutal crime, for a reparation of which the moment has come." [12] To support the "missions" of these representatives the Polish National Committee began to publish books, periodicals, and pamphlets which tortured history to prove that the partitions of Poland were the greatest crimes in the history of the world and that, significantly enough, Germany and Austria were the chief criminals.[13] These publications soon began to exert influence in all the capitals of the Allied Powers.[14]

8. It must be remembered that the minority groups, though organizationally weaker, were composed of skilled workers including miners.

9. See below, Chapter 7.

10. The Polish National Committee was formed in August 1914 in response to the proclamation of the supreme commander of the Russian forces which promised Polish autonomy "under the sceptre of His Imperial Majesty." The committee remained faithful to the Russian Imperial Government when after the Bolshevik Revolution it transferred its headquarters to Paris. In September 1918 France and Great Britain recognized the Polish National Committee as the supreme Polish authority. The United States did the same in November 1918. See Filasiewicz, *La Question polonaise*, pp. 380–1, 575.

11. Landau, *Paderewski*, p. 109.

12. *Ibid.*

13. See Paderewski, "Poland's So-called Corridor," *Foreign Affairs, 11* (1933), 421. See also above, Chapter 1.

14. Even the very cautious Secretary of State Lansing was soon affected by

To the Polish National Committee the United States was of the utmost importance in any Polish propaganda. In no other country outside Poland were there so many Poles.[15] No other country could supply so much money to prepare the Polish cause and to relieve the devastated, war-stricken country. The voice of neutral America would have weight with other countries. Paderewski abandoned his musical career to devote himself to this work, to become propagandist, orator, diplomat, and statesman.

He was admirably fitted for his mission in the United States; his name was more famous than that of any other foreign artist, and many of the country's leaders were his friends. He made several trips to America as the official representative of the Polish National Committee, delivered speeches at Polish benefit meetings in universities, clubs, concert halls and theaters, and addressed crowds large and small. The tickets were expensive; the money was collected ostensibly for Polish charities. He would speak for almost half an hour, stating Poland's case, and afterward play Polish music, mainly Chopin. In all his speeches he coupled the name of Poland with the future victory of the Allies. "That aroused the people's emotions, showing them another aspect of the problem. Paderewski gave over 300 of these concerts combined with speeches, and after each of them the cause of Poland was a little advanced." [16]

For a majority of American citizens the name of Poland soon became synonymous with the name of Paderewski.[17] His political declarations were reproduced conspicuously in the American press, which always took them for authoritative statements. Even the German ambassador in Washington, Count Bernstorff, commented in a letter to Chancellor Bethmann-Hollweg on how well informed

---

this propaganda. He wrote: "The dismemberment of so large and populous a territory possessing solidarity in race, language, and religion, such as Poland possessed was an international crime which hardly finds a parallel in the annals of the past four hundred years. . . ." Robert Lansing, *The Big Four and Others of the Peace Conference* (Boston and New York, Houghton Mifflin, 1921), pp. 197–8.

15. Polish leaders asserted that in 1914 there were four million Poles in America. This assertion was extravagant. According to the U.S. census of 1910 there were 1,684,108 native as well as foreign-born Poles who spoke Polish. By 1920 the Polish-speaking population had climbed to 2,436,895. The census of 1930 shows 3,342,198 Poles in America. This figure, which was not based solely on the Polish language, included foreign- as well as native-born Poles who had one or more parents born in Poland.

16. Landau, *Paderewski*, pp. 110–11.

17. "Never before in the history of America," wrote Landau, "was the name of Poland so widely known as it now became through the efforts of Paderewski." *Ibid.*, p. 111.

the American press was about all Polish matters, and attributed it to Paderewski's activities.[18]

Paderewski's appointment as leader of Polish-American opinion apparently misled his friend Colonel House who, though sincerely concerned with the Polish cause, did not look further into the nature of Paderewski's position among the Polish-Americans. In "Paderewski: The Paradox of Europe" House wrote:

> When Paderewski reached America, the entire situation under his direction was immediately changed. He gave to the American Poles a single purpose, checking all futile and scattered desires. . . . Having foreseen before others the part the United States was to play in the great tragedy, . . . Paderewski never lost faith in the ultimate outcome . . . In what measure the efforts and sagacity of Paderewski were crowned by success may be gauged by the fact that toward the close of 1916 his countrymen in America, without dissent, chose him as their plenipotentiary, conferring upon him power of attorney to act for them and decide all political matters in their name and on their behalf [sic]. . . . Paderewski encouraged Polish youth to enter officers' training schools, and presently he brought about the foundation of a Polish organization for the training of officers. Finally, when the United States entered the war, he sounded an eloquent call to arms. . . .[19]

To the majority of American Poles, Paderewski was not a representative of Poland; he was only an agent of the pro-Russian bloc. At the time of the pianist's activities in the United States the Poles in America were divided into three antagonistic groups. One followed Pilsudski, who was then organizing Polish legions in Austrian Poland to fight Russia. His principle, "Russia is the first enemy to be fought . . . destroy her and then try to win over Austria and Germany," was adopted by the leading Poles in America. They formed a Committee of National Defense at Pittsburgh, which included representatives from all the most important and most influential Polish-American societies. It pledged itself to "assist by all means the revolutionary movement against Russia, the greatest enemy of Poland." [20] Early in 1916 it merged

18. Count Bernstorff, *My Three Years in America* (New York, 1920), p. 349.
19. House, "Paderewski: The Paradox of Europe," *Harper's Magazine, 152* (1925), 30.
20. Anon., "America and Polish Politics," *New Republic, 17* (1918), 38–40.

with a newly organized Alliance of Polish Socialists which professed to be a branch of the Polish Socialist party of Pilsudski.
Like the parent body it was intensely nationalistic and its principal object in America was to help the Central Powers and prepare its members to participate in the political and social life of a
restored Poland. The Committee of National Defense (called
K.O.N. from the Polish initials of its title) looked forward to a
Polish republic with a democratic form of government and a moderate socialistic policy in industrial matters. In foreign policies
it was strongly anti-Russian and inclined toward Austria from
whom it hoped to receive political and cultural autonomy but not
complete independence. As a group it soon came under suspicion
in the United States partly because of its pro-German attitude but
primarily because of the accusations of Paderewski's followers.[21]
It was charged with favoring the defeat of Russia, with being pro-
German, and with opposing the recruitment of an independent
Polish army in the United States.[22]

The second group was composed of followers of Dmowski and
Paderewski. Its leaders talked freely about a future Poland with
a population of 30 or even 35 million, a number that could not pos-
sibly be reached without annexing large numbers of non-Polish
elements. It was primarily because of this aim that the members
of this group began to press, as soon as they had a following
among the American Poles, for the recruitment of soldiers for a
Polish army in America. The purpose in this was not, as many believed, to give the Polish National Committee a stronger voice in
the Peace Council but to prepare for conquering territory as soon
as hostilities ended.[23] This party even as late as September 1918
wanted a strong Polish monarchy and conceived of Poland chiefly
as a buffer state between Russia and Germany.[24] It also looked forward to the re-establishment of a monarchy, though not the

21. The Polish newspaper *Wici,* which opposed the Paderewski group, had this
to say: "Everywhere . . . in Maspeth, Long Island, in Harrison, New Jersey, in
Bridgeport, Connecticut, in Hartford, Connecticut, Northampton, Massachusetts,
and in many other American cities, including New York and Chicago . . . Polish
parasites intercept American authorities from the policemen to the Secretary of
State, and throw false calumnies against the Poles. 'Catch, arrest, the members of
K.O.N., for they are German spies, enemies of America, pacifists, I.W.W.'s, terrors
of the universe, cosmic dangers.'" *Wici,* Mar. 26, 1918. Quoted by Park, *Immigrant
Press,* p. 204.
22. After the United States gave permission to recruit Poles, their opposition
ceased.
23. See below, Chapter 11.
24. House diary, Sept. 14, 1918. See below, p. 98.

tsardom, in Russia, and expected Poland to be, if not directly under the influence of Russia, at least closely allied to it. Principally through Dmowski's good standing with the previous Russian Government on account of his Russophile policy, he and his followers were able to establish friendly relations in Paris and London and eventually acquire official status. When the Paris Committee of the National Democratic party extended its power to America, it began to agitate against United States neutrality and for early American participation in the European war.

The imperialistic and conservative ideology of the Polish National Committee appealed to many Poles in America. Soon after Paderewski arrived, he succeeded in winning over the Polish National Alliance and the Roman Catholic Union to his program.[25] Both of these organizations, which numbered 230,000 members between them, accepted the pro-Russian policy of the National Committee and gave it financial and political support.

To the third group belonged those American Poles, primarily of the second and third generation, who resented the propaganda of both the pro-Russian and pro-German Poles. They considered themselves Americans and not Poles or even Polish Americans. "As Americans," wrote Jan Kobiet,

> we do not wish to build an isolated Polishism in this country. We wish our sons to fight side by side with their fellow citizens. . . .
>
> As Poles, we also want our men to be in the American army. What weight will Poland have in the Peace Councils because of an army, probably disbanded, of a few thousand men compared with the force exercised by President Wilson when the American army shall have brought victory over Germany? . . . And we believe that so far as the policy of the Paris Committee of Poles is allowed to determine the decisions regarding Poland, so far will the weight incline again in favor of the old politics of balance of power, imperialism and reactionism.[26]

25. The Polish National Alliance accepted the theory that the Polish immigrants in America should form an autonomous part of the Polish nation through superterritorial organization of federated local groups. The early promoters of this organization believed that although the Poles in America might become deeply involved in American life they still could be kept as a part of the Polish nation. It was this group that Paderewski recognized as the official representative of Polish Americans.

26. Jan Kobiet, "America and the Polish Question," *New Republic, 16* (1918),

This group was angered by those Poles who regarded Polish immigrants in America as the "fourth part of Poland." They vigorously opposed the European Poles' attempt to control the American immigrant and the American Poles' desire to control Europe. Throughout the war years their press denounced this attempt of the American colony to interfere in America's and Poland's affairs. One of their newspapers, the *Telegram Codzienny*, stated:

We have here among the immigrants a good-sized group of our political "great men" who are very much puffed up and very pugnacious, and as a result thereof very ridiculous. . . .

These are the same people who . . . are on the one hand unwilling to recognize the world-leadership of America in this war, and on the other hand are striving to impose upon Poland their political leadership and rule Poland from outside Polish territory.

These . . . people . . . are for the most part still very "green" among us, and who have very poor and superficial notions as to conditions prevailing among us. They all fight against windmills, and they all think they are Poles and famous men, and that they alone are the only ones called upon to save Poland.[27]

In their attacks on the Polish political agitators they pointed out that most of the "four million" Poles in America were engaged in war industries and hence they asked the United States Government to scrutinize carefully the character, methods, and objectives of the Polish organizations in America.[28] Above all the group feared and hated the antiliberal Polish National Committee. They felt that Paderewski represented an organization whose reaction-

---

46. The same reaction of the second- and third-generation American Poles was noticed in the second World War. According to Dr. Karol Wachtl even first-generation immigrants who came to America before World War II did not show much interest in joining the Polish army in England that was to fight against Germany to help free Poland. A good many of the refugees and dignitaries from Poland were not even interested enough to recruit for the cause. The younger Americans of the third and fourth generation, he declared, had no enthusiasm for Polish nationalism at all. See Wachtl, *Polonja*, pp. 420–2.

27. Quoted by Park, *Immigrant Press*, p. 202.

28. Irwin Edman, "The Fourth Part of Poland," *Nation*, 107 (1918), 342. The United States Government did investigate the charges of this group. In the summer of 1918, at the request of Major Hunt of the Military Intelligence Bureau, John Dewey prepared a report for President Wilson which described the conditions among the Poles in America. See Dewey to Wilson, Sept. 25, 1918, Wilson MSS.

ary character injured the Polish cause and augured ill for the quality of freedom which Poland was to possess after the war.[29]

29. "Paderewski," wrote the *Dziennik Ludowy*, "who had little success in Europe as composer of the Opera 'Manru,' began a happier role yesterday as hero of a comic operetta. . . . Paderewski spoke for Poland, although that country has announced through all official and semi-official organs that Paderewski has no mandate from Poland at all. . . . Mr. Helenski . . . who was appointed as the representative of American Poles at a secret meeting composed of fifteen self-named representatives of Polish insurance societies who were neither requested nor entitled to represent anybody . . . spoke and laid at the feet of the master a tribute from the four million Poles in America." *Dziennik Ludowy*, Chicago, Mar. 4, 1918.

5. Wilson and the Polish-Americans

THREE IMPORTANT FACTORS counterbalanced the division among American Poles and helped Paderewski carry out his political activities. The first was the change in Wilson's feeling toward American Poles, the second was the American relief program, and the last was Paderewski's friendship with influential Americans.

Politics does strange things to professors and statesmen. Before the first World War Professor Wilson had little but contempt for the Polish-Americans. In his own hastily written *History of the American People,* published in 1902, he even advocated a reduction of Polish immigration to the United States. His uncomplimentary opinion of the Poles in America is plain from the following passage:

> . . . but now there came multitudes of men of lowest class from the south of Italy and men of the meaner sort out of Hungary and Poland, men out of the ranks where there was neither skill nor energy nor any initiative of quick intelligence; and they came in numbers which increased from year to year, as if the countries of the south of Europe were disburdening themselves of the more sordid and hapless elements of their population, the men whose standard of life and of work were such as American workmen had never dreamed of hitherto.[1]

Then, as if to add insult to injury, Wilson compared the Chinese to the "new" immigrants in the following terms: ". . . yet the Chinese were more to be desired, as workmen if not as citizens, than most of the coarse crew that came crowding in every year at the eastern ports."[2]

The passage was written in 1902, at a time when Wilson interested himself in academic life and scholarship. In 1912 his long-nursed ambition for the presidency was closer to realization. He now took pains to purge himself of his careless historical rhetoric of a decade earlier—the derogatory remarks about the Polish-Americans. Polish votes were more important than lively writing.

Wilson's early attitude toward American Poles would probably

1. Woodrow Wilson, *A History of the American People* (New York, Harper, 1902), *5,* 212–13.
2. *Ibid.*

have gone unnoticed had it not been for studious political opponents in the anti-Wilson press who used the passages from his *History* to discredit the ambitious governor of New Jersey. On May 27, 1912, the New York *Evening Journal* opened its attack on Wilson by stating: "Professor Wilson is on record as an advocate of Chinese labor. He has declared over his own signature that he considers the Chinaman, with all his vices, preferable to white immigrants from Southern Europe—Italians, Hungarians, Poles, et cetera." [3]

The press made Wilson's opinion about Polish immigrants a matter of public knowledge. Immediately Polish societies began to organize vociferous opposition. "As Mr. Wilson has shown that he is narrow and unjust in his attitude toward the Poles . . . ," reads a resolution adopted by the United Polish Societies of Manhattan, "we, Polish American citizens of the United Polish Societies, strongly and unanimously oppose his possible nomination." [4] All over the country Polish priests were admonishing their parishioners to vote against Wilson. "What he says is an insult to the white race," declared the Reverend John H. Strzelecki of St. Stanislaw's Church. [5] "Attention, Polish American Citizens," read a widely distributed Polish pamphlet, "Woodrow Wilson insulted you. Are you going to vote for your slanderer? Read carefully, and decide." [6]

Realizing that this opposition might hurt his chances for nomination, Wilson began to make desperate attempts to explain away his calumnies. He wrote to Polish leaders professing his great admiration and love for the "new immigrants." To F. Ignatius Drobinski, a Polish leader, he wrote: "I yield to no one in my admiration of the Polish character. I have received the greatest stimulation from my reading of Polish history [!]. [7] If my terms

3. Cited by Arthur S. Link, *Wilson: The Road to the White House* (Princeton, Princeton University Press, 1947), 383–90.

4. *Ibid.*

5. *Ibid.*

6. This pamphlet was distributed by a committee of the publishers of the foreign press in America, which claimed that it represented more than 120 publications. In Congress Representative William A. Rodenberg of Illinois attacked Wilson for his antiforeign attitude. The speech of the Congressman, including excerpts from Wilson's *History of the American People,* was translated into Polish, Czech, Yiddish, Italian, and other languages and distributed among various national groups.

7. Even at the Peace Conference, when one would assume that President Wilson should have known at least some aspect of Polish history, Clemenceau was shocked when discussing "a bit of history" with Wilson to learn how little he knew about Poland and its people. See Stephen Bonsal, *Suitors and Suppliants: The Little Nations at Versailles* (New York, Prentice-Hall, 1946), p. 110.

WAŻNE DLA
Obywateli
Polaków.

Woodrow Wilson
ubliżył wam!

Czy oddacie głos swemu oszczercy?

Czytajcie uważnie; zastanówcie się,

ROZSTRZYGNIJCIE SAMI!

Propaganda leaflet urging the Poles not to vote for Wilson

Woodrow Wilson

Präsidentschaftskandidat der Einwanderungsfeinde.

Wilson gegen die eingewanderten Bürger.

Herr Vorsitzender: Ich stand unter dem Eindruck, daß der Geist des „Knownothing"tums, der einst dieses Land durchseuchte, längst tot sei. Ich stand unter dem Eindruck, daß dieser Geist für immer aus der Welt vertrieben sei durch die überzeugende Kraft der großen Wahrheit, welche die festeste Grundlage unserer republikanischen Regierungsform bildet, daß „alle Menschen frei und gleich vor ihrem Schöpfer mit gewissen unveräußerlichen Rechten begabt, geschaffen sind." Ich habe nicht geglaubt, daß jemals die Zeit kommen würde, wo eine große politische Partei als ihren Präsidentschaftskandidaten einen Mann aufstellen würde, bei dem noch eine Spur der Unduldsamkeit des Vorurteils und der engherzigen Abneigung übrig geblieben scheint, welche jener unamerikanischen fremdenfeindlichen Agitation vor 50 Jahren Leben gab.

Auf S. 212 Bd. 5 von Woodrow Wilsons „Geschichte des amerikanischen Volkes" finde ich folgenden bemerkenswerten Ausdruck:

„Jetzt aber kamen Massen von Menschen der niedrigsten Klassen aus Süditalien und Menschen der gemeineren Sorte aus Ungarn und Polen, Menschen aus jenen Schichten, wo es weder Geschicklichkeit noch Arbeitskraft, noch irgend welche Regsamkeit lebhaften Geistes gab. Und sie kamen in einer Anzahl, die von Jahr zu Jahr wuchs, als ob die Länder Südeuropas sich der schmutzigeren, elenderen Bestandteile ihrer Bevölkerung entledigten. Männer, deren Lebenshaltung und Arbeit eine solche war, wie sie sich der amerikanische

---

Woodrow Wilson

PROTI

přistěhovalým občanům.

Nezapomeňte, že hlas pro Roosevelta znamená hlas pro Wilsona – a Wilson napsal následující:

"Ted' ale přicházely massy lidí nejnižší třídy z jižní Italie a lidé sprostšího druhu z Uher a Polska, lidé z oněch vrstev, u nichž nebylo ani obratnosti ani pracovní zdatnosti, ani nějaké čilosti živého ducha. – A přicházely v takovém počtu, jenž rok od roku rostl, jakoby země jižní Evropy zbavovaly se nejšpinavější a nejhorší části svého obyvatelstva. Mužové. jejichž způsob života a práce byly takového druhu, o jakých se americkým dělníkům nikdy předtím nesnilo. — —

Číňané byli žádoucnější jako dělníci. když ne jako občani, nežli většina této hrubé hordy, jež se rok od roku hromadila v našich východních přístavech."

(Z "Dějin amerického národa," svazek V., stránka 212.)

Woodrow Wilson

CONTRO

I cittadini Forestieri.

Ricordate che un voto per Roosevelt é un voto per Wilson — l'uomo che scrisse:

Vennero molt'tudini di nomini delle classi piu basse dall'Italia Meridionale e nomini della peggiore qualità dall'Ungheria e dalla Polonia, nomini che vennero fuori quelle cassi dove non vi era né abilità, né energia, ne qualsiasi iniziativa d'intelligenza.

Questi vennero in numero che accrebbero di anno in anno come se la nazione dell'Europa meridionale stassero sbarazzando degli elementi piu sordidi e inabili dalle loro popolazioni, ai quali il modo di vita e di lavoro erano tali che il lavoro Americano non avevano mai prima sognato.

I cinesi erano piu desiderabili come lovoratori se non come cittadini, anziché la maggior parte della ciurma sozza che ogni anno venne ad affollare i porti dell'est.

Storia del Popolo Americano Volume 5 Pag. 212.

וואָדראָו וויִלסאָן

געגען־ארבייטער און פאר־קינעזער קאנדידאט פאר פרעזידענט.

וויִלסאָן דער פריינד פון קינעזער.

פאראעטשאר וויִלסאָן, וויִ עס ווייזט אויס, האָט שטארק ליעב
דעם כינעזער, פארשטאענדיג דעם אויסזאָג, וואָס איך דאָ
יעצט געברענג, אויף זיינע זייטע 213, בוך 5, פון וואָדראָו וויִלסאָנ'ס
"געשיכטע פון דער אמעריקאנער נאציאָן", זאָגט דער פראַע־
זאר וויִלסער ווי פאָלגט:

"איצט מיונעגליער די כינעזער
האָבען אהן צווייפעל געהאַט פיעלע אונאַנגענעהמ'ל זיטען, האָ־
בעדאָרט אויסגענאַרדאעוונגס זיך בייא די אוננגזוינדע אַנגעזאָפקט
ים־ברעגען פון מערק, און עס האָם אויסגעזויבערב, אַז עס מיט דער זייר
שען, צווישען וועלכע זיי זיינען געקומען לעבען.

אבער דאָס וואָס איז געווען זייער קענטשאאפט, זייער אינדעפליגענץ,
זייער שטארקער כח צו ארבייטען, זייער פעחיקייט צו מאַכען
א בוקעט און ארומסעוטרויבען שנעאבער קאָנקורעטזאָן, און
גים זיידעלע אמעריקאנישע זיטען, פאר וואָס מען האָם זאר זיי
מורא געהאַט און פיינע געקראַגען און וואָס האָם געפיהרט צו
זייער פערשיכסונג. נאַמען שוין אונגעויטידען זיי זיין פון די יעניגע,
וועלכע האָבען מורא געקראַגען, אָז די כינעזער וועלען פערנעאעט־
מען זייערע פלעצער, אויב זיי וועלען זיך דאַ פערמעהרען. די
אונגעגונשטינסטע מענשען, וועלכע זיינען געקומען אין די פאַרטס
פון דער אוסם, זיינען שאַלעריאָם גענואּרען נור דעראָאר, ווייל
דאָס האָבען זיך געקומען צו די נידערינגסטע שאַרואָג ארבייטער."

מר. שעערמאַן, די היסטאָריער פון דעם גיערי עקט, וועל־
קער איז דורכגענאנגען אין 1892, און וועלכער האָם געפאַדרט
צו דער אויסשליסונג פון כינעזער פון די יוניטעטר סטייטס,
דערעכטהיילט אונז, אַז דער עקט איז דורכגענאאָרען געוואָרען אויף
דעם איינשטימיגען פאַרלאנג פון די אמעריקא־

were too sweeping they must be attributed to my clumsiness in expressing myself." [8] Wilson clumsy in expression! His defense must have sounded absurd to those who knew him, read his works, or listened to his speeches. Even Lansing, who put little faith in Wilson's abilities, had to admit that "with fluency and with perfect diction he [Wilson] would present his views in sentences so well rounded that they suggested copper-plate perfection. His accuracy of language and his positiveness of assertion not infrequently reminded one of a lecturer imparting knowledge to a class." [9] But in another letter to a Polish-American leader Wilson, perhaps realizing the weakness of the former excuse, stated that he "referred in his *History* only to laborers who were brought to America under contract." [10]

The climax in Wilson's "great apology" came when a Polish-American group in New York suggested that he insert an erratum slip in his book retracting his derogatory remarks and rewrite the passage in the next edition. They also wanted him to make a public apology to Americans of Polish, Italian, and Hungarian birth and descent. "There was a time," Link wrote, "when Wilson would have hastened to rebuke such 'impudence'; now, however, he was a politician and quaffed the bitter draught." [11] He ignored two of the requests. Then he replied: "I think with you that it would be best for me at the earliest possible moment to rewrite the passage referred to in my history. I shall get into communication with my publishers and ascertain the feasibility of doing this at an earlier date." [12] Shortly after this reply Wilson did inform his publishers that he would like to reconsider and rewrite certain passages "in order to remove the false impressions which they seemed to have made." But when, after his election in 1916, the new edition appeared the passage was still there.[13]

It is doubtful if Wilson's belated apology had any important bearing on the election of 1912. No work has yet appeared analyzing the Polish vote for that year. The only information available concerns the Polish priests, who voted overwhelmingly for Theodore Roosevelt. A canvass of 2213 Catholic priests made on October

8. Link, *Wilson,* pp. 383–90.
9. Lansing, *The Big Four,* p. 59.
10. Link, *Wilson,* pp. 383–90.
11. *Ibid.*
12. *Ibid.*
13. Woodrow Wilson, *A History of the American People* (2d ed. New York, Harper and Brothers, 1917), *10,* 98.

12, 1912, by National Democratic Party Headquarters revealed that of the Polish priests 70 per cent were for Roosevelt. Of the 59 Polish priests who polled, 18 were for Wilson, 4 for Taft, and 37 for Roosevelt. The poll also showed that the majority of the German Franciscan Fathers supported Wilson, whereas the Polish and Italian Franciscans were overwhelmingly for Roosevelt and Taft. A majority of the Polish Catholic press favored Roosevelt.[14] One cannot, of course, infer from the above that the Poles in America voted as did their priests. Nevertheless the Democratic party, it is important to realize, felt that these priests exerted an important influence on the votes of their parishioners. In all probability the decisive factor in the election of Wilson was the split in the Republican party which enabled the Democrats with a minority of popular votes to assume control of the national government.[15]

In 1916 the Democrats viewed the coming presidential election with considerable uncertainty. Wilson's prestige was at its lowest ebb. Criticism within the party was mounting. The mending of the breach that had occurred in the Republican party in 1912 made the task of the Democrats formidable. On June 26, 1916, as a result of Roosevelt's endorsement of Hughes, unity between the stalwarts and the progressives was achieved, and the Republicans gained a distinct advantage in the forthcoming election.

As soon as the nominations were made, the general lines of the campaign became apparent. In the East the trend of popular opinion was against the president; his handling of the Mexican situation was criticized; and it was generally felt that he had not been strong enough against Germany. The Republicans therefore felt sure of the East and turned their primary attention to the West. They concentrated on capturing the progressive vote and on exploiting the antipathies of the German-Americans toward Wilson. The Democrats realized that they had little chance in the East and that the battle would be in the West to capture progressives and independents. In order to offset the German-American dislike of Wilson they began to cultivate those Americans of foreign extraction whose native countries had been overrun by the German Empire.

In the latter campaign tactic the Democrats were actually helped by Theodore Roosevelt's speeches. His vigorous public addresses attacking hyphenated Americans embarrassed Hughes

14. James A. O'Gorman to James K. McGuire, Oct. 12, 1912, Wilson MSS.
15. See Appendix.

and made his efforts to satisfy German-Americans more difficult. Roosevelt not only helped the Democrats in their endeavor to gain the support of Americans of foreign origin but also scared many German-Americans away from Hughes.[16]

It is perhaps no mere coincidence that soon after his renomination President Wilson took a firm stand against requiring literacy tests of immigrants coming to the United States. In 1902 Professor Wilson had been much upset by the mean sort of immigrants coming to America out of Hungary and Poland, who had "neither skill nor energy nor any initiative of quick intelligence." Now he wanted to help the countries of Europe to disburden themselves "of the more sordid and hapless elements of their population." Polish organizations were, of course, much impressed with his new attitude and began to write him letters of thanks and support. Roman L. Modra, president of the Polish-American Democratic League, informed Wilson that his organization, representing a great majority of Polish-American voters in the eastern states, unanimously and "in glowing terms" endorsed his re-election. He concluded by stating: "I beg to add that you have solidified the great Polish-American vote in the United States through your fair treatment of all American citizens of foreign extraction. The differences of opinion among our voters which existed in 1912 has [sic] been practically wiped out and we assure you that the great majority will vote solidly for you." [17] Even some local Democratic politicians who depended on the Polish vote soon let their party leader know that his stand against the literacy test was a great political strategem. One "literate" postmaster, E. A. Purdy of Minneapolis, wrote to Wilson: "The Polish people seem to have a

16. "It would be beneficial for the President," Daniel C. Roper, chairman of the Democratic National Committee, wrote to House, "to refer again to what he means by hyphenated Americans and draw his former distinction clearly between them and other of foreign birth or extraction, and in this connection refer to Roosevelt's position in the campaign as the spokesman of Mr. Hughes, in which he practically denounces all Germans, and defend the 'Americanized' Germans, which is the great body of them, against Roosevelt's sweeping aspersions. . . ." Roper to House, Oct. 7, 1916, Wilson MSS. House questioned the advisability of Roper's suggestion.

17. Roman L. Modra to Wilson, Aug. 24, 1916, Wilson MSS. Ignatius Werwinski, in a letter to Tumulty asking for an autographed photo of Wilson for the Polish Women's Alliance Museum, made this interesting statement: "This organization also has its own newspaper, which is very influential and carries quite a weight. I think if the President would consent to this little favor, he would be helped quite a good deal in his present campaign, and would secure the co-operation of this organization." Werwinski to Tumulty, Aug. 14, 1916, Wilson MSS.

certain knowledge of what peace and freedom mean. . . . The Polish people are very much opposed, and I believe rightly, to the Literecy [sic] Test." [18]

Wilson's "great apology" and his stand against the literacy test did win him many friends.[19] It was not, however, until the summer of 1916 that the Polish-Americans became sure of Wilson's change of heart. What brought this about was his sincere endeavor to help the war sufferers of Europe.

At the time Paderewski arrived in the United States, American humanitarian sympathies were already aroused. During the late months of 1915 the American press published reports from Belgium, Poland, and other countries, pointing out the need for relief to the starving people of Europe. Germany was removing food from Belgium, thus jeopardizing the continuance of British consent for the Belgian Relief Committee to send food to Belgium. The same practice also tended to prevent giving relief to Poland. As the battle lines moved eastward so did the devastation. Villages and crops were destroyed. Factories closed, throwing industrial populations out of work and leaving them helpless and in distress. There were no animals for transport, no agricultural implements, no seed. The occupying powers monopolized and requisitioned all products of the soil. Famine attacked millions of adults and children all over occupied Poland. American reports, investigations, and diplomatic intervention had no effect whatever.[20] The warring powers sought to place moral responsibility for the failure upon each other, and Poland was denied large-scale relief from America until the Armistice.

Although these negotiations failed to accomplish their object

18. E. A. Purdy to Wilson, May 8, 1916, Wilson MSS.

19. As if to test Wilson's change in attitude, Polish newspapers in America began to investigate whether he had appointed any Polish-Americans to government positions after his nomination in 1912. Representative A. J. Sabath wrote to Tumulty: "I am in communication with the Polish News Papers and would like to secure from you the names of any Polish American citizens that have been named by President Wilson in any of the States in addition to Mr. Smietenka who has [sic] appointed in Chicago as Internal Revenue Collector." Sabath to Tumulty, Mar. 23, 1916, Wilson MSS. Wilson ordered an immediate inquiry. On March 30 he was informed by Acting Secretary of the Interior Jones that the inquiry made of all departments "found only one man Joseph Winczewski, Registrar ? of the Land Office at Duluth, Minnesota. . . ." The only Polish-American appointed upon the nomination of Wilson "was born 1867 or 68 on ocean en route to United States from Poland." Jones to Wilson, Mar. 30, 1916, Wilson MSS.

20. Hartley Notter, *The Origins of the Foreign Policy of Woodrow Wilson* (Baltimore, 1937), pp. 511–12 and 551–2. See also Ray Stannard Baker, *Woodrow Wilson: Life and Letters* (New York, Doubleday, Doran, 1927–46), *6*, 336–44.

they inevitably directed attention to Poland's political situation. Sympathy for war sufferers merged with sympathy for Polish demands for unity and some kind of independence for the nation. Large numbers of Americans were anxious about the welfare of the Polish people, and the State Department was forced to press negotiations for relief to these victims.[21] Herbert Hoover and Frederic Walcott of the Rockefeller Foundation drafted relief plans; but the British Foreign Office was adamant in requiring that the industrial part of Poland controlled by Austria-Hungary be treated as a unit so that the starving people conquered by Germany could be supplied from the farms controlled by Austria-Hungary. The Central Powers were also required to refrain from using food from any part of Poland. Although these demands were not heeded and hopes for relief were frustrated, the United States Department of State continued to plead with Germany that disagreements over details should not be allowed to condemn the Polish people to continued starvation.[22] All this was in vain.

The hopeless situation did not diminish President Wilson's humanitarian zeal. In December 1915 he set aside the first day of January 1916 as a day for American citizens to collect funds to help Polish victims.[23] According to Hartley Notter, Wilson was continuously "striving to gain the co-operation of the belligerents in relieving distress among Polish peoples." [24] On December 21, 1915, the Polish National Council wrote to President Wilson: "To his excellency we beg leif to express our deepest gratitude for your noble minded interest in the Polish cause and your note worthy desires to support our war stricken brethren in Poland. The Poles shall never forget this significant humanitarian act of President Wilson." [25]

From all over the country letters and telegrams poured into the White House thanking Wilson for his unselfish zeal and interest. Paderewski, plenipotentiary of the Paris Committee and ex officio head of all the major activities of the Poles, including relief, sent him a wire: "In behalf of stricken Polan I beg of your excellency to accept with the homage of deepest respect the expression

21. Lansing to Page, Feb. 26, 1916, *FR: 1916,* Supplement, p. 887.

22. Page to Secretary of State, Feb. 28, 1916, *ibid.;* see also Notter, *The Origins of the Foreign Policy of Woodrow Wilson,* pp. 511–12.

23. Paderewski to Wilson, Dec. 24, 1915, Wilson MSS.

24. See also Page to Secretary of State, Feb. 28, 1916, *FR: 1916,* Supplement, p. 887.

25. Polish National Council to Wilson, Dec. 21, 1915, Wilson MSS.

of most profound gratitude for your truly magnamious action." [26]

Wilson's efforts to help the European peoples became more vigorous as the presidential elections approached. On July 7, 1916, he asked the State Department to issue a circular appeal to the governments of the Allied and Central Powers requesting them "in the name of and interest of humanity" to see to it that the innocent Polish population should not suffer starvation.[27] While awaiting replies Wilson told a delegation of Polish-American citizens: "I know the terrible conditions, the tragical conditions, that exist there, and nobody could know them without feeling his heart torn with the knowledge." [28]

As appeals from the Polish organizations increased Wilson became more and more interested. On July 13, 1916, he wrote to the undersecretary of State, Frank L. Polk, that a "very earnest appeal" had been made to him by representatives

> of our fellow citizens of Polish blood. . . . I would like your very candid advice as to whether it would be wise or in any way efficacious . . . for me to address personal letters to the King of England, the Emperor of Germany, the Emperor of Austria, the Czar of Russia, and the President of France, appealing to them to cooperate with us in making arrangements which will enable the Polish citizens of the United States to send food to their suffering friends and kinsmen in Poland. That is the only thing I can think of that we have not yet done.[29]

On July 20, 1916, reassured by Polk and no longer willing to rely upon State Department officials, Wilson addressed personal letters to the heads of the governments concerned. In these he wrote that he "felt justified by the universal . . . expression of the sympathies of the American people . . . to suggest a fresh consideration of the means for saving the starving people." [30] It was in his campaign speeches, however, that Wilson gave fullest consideration to the problem of relief. "The only thing that moves

26. Paderewski to Wilson, Dec. 24, 1915, Wilson MSS.

27. Lansing to American Ambassadors, *FR: 1916,* Supplement, pp. 899–900 and 886–913.

28. Baker, *Woodrow Wilson, 6,* 339.

29. Wilson to Polk, July 13, 1916, quoted in Baker, *Woodrow Wilson, 6,* 340.

30. *FR:* July 21, 1916, Supplement, pp. 903–4. Wilson received personal answers from all the heads of the belligerent states. See *FR: 1916,* Supplement, pp. 905–7, 909, and 912. See also *FR: Lansing Papers, 1,* 686–7 and 692. His failure in regard to Polish relief was announced publicly on Oct. 18, 1916, in the *New York Times.*

life," he said on October 7, with the national election less than a month away, "is the impulse of the heart . . . by the kind of things which bring men together. . . . We were born to prefer justice to power, humanity to any form of selfish achievement." [31] Shortly thereafter he named special days for giving relief to Armenians, Syrians, and Lithuanians,[32] but not for Polish relief. Doubtless that would have been too obvious a political gesture: his political opponents would have done their best to turn it against him. Instead, he delicately reminded the Polish-American voters (October 26, 1916) of their "weakness" in being "unorganized." [33] This is the first time—so far as the author of these pages knows— that an American president has gone to the length of suggesting that hyphenated American citizens organize for political purposes. And these citizens were the sons of that "coarse crew" of Polish immigrants who had been crowding into our eastern seaports at the turn of the century! Just as Paderewski wanted to organize the Polish-Americans for his own political purposes, so Wilson would have liked to see them organized for his: the re-election of Woodrow Wilson as president of the United States of America. A short time after his strong hint for Polish-American unity in backing his campaign, Wilson allowed House and Paderewski to persuade him that the latter had in effect power of attorney to act for Polish-Americans and decide all political matters for them in their name. Recognizing Paderewski as head of the Poles in America would be a way of keeping Wilson at the head of Polish-American voters in the United States.

According to Landau, "Paderewski's influence made practically all the Poles in the States vote for Wilson, and even the partly Republican Catholic Clergy among the Poles voted for the Democratic Wilson. As was later shown," Landau asserted, "the Democrats in three big states won a victory through the vote of the Poles." [34]

A detailed examination of the election returns shows that Wilson won by a combination of western and southern votes. Of primary importance, however, was the President's victory in four Midwest-

31. *New York Times,* Oct. 8, 1916.
32. *Ibid.,* Sept. 9, 1916.
33. Speech in Cincinnati, incompletely reported, *ibid.,* Oct. 27, 1916. Paderewski took the hint and chose a very appropriate day, Nov. 6, 1916, the eve of the Presidential election, when the American Poles were being "organized" to vote for Wilson, to ask the president to set aside a day to help the Poles.
34. Landau, *Paderewski,* p. 115.

ern states: Ohio, Missouri, North Dakota, and Kansas. In these four states the Polish vote seems to have overwhelmingly favored the president.[35] In the region north of the Ohio River and east of the Mississippi Hughes carried every state except New Hampshire and Ohio. Wilson's plurality in New Hampshire was only 56 votes, but in Ohio it was 90,408. Hughes carried only two border states, Delaware and West Virginia, and only four states—Minnesota, Wisconsin, South Dakota, and Oregon—in the Midwest and West. While Landau failed to name the three states he referred to, and offered no proof of his assertion, it is likely that the Polish vote in Ohio, Missouri, North Dakota, and Kansas was an important contributing factor in Wilson's re-election.

It has been commonly stated that the failure of Hiram Johnson to support Hughes in California lost the election for the Republicans. A more tactful handling of the California problem might have brought that state into the Republican fold. But even with a fair margin of votes in California, Hughes would still have had a minority of the popular vote of the nation. Thus it seems more reasonable to suppose that Wilson's victory in the four Midwestern states was responsible for the return of the Democrats to power.

35. See Appendix.

6. Wilson, House, and Paderewski

IN ACCORDANCE WITH the instructions of the National Democratic party Paderewski, as soon as he arrived in the United States, began to cultivate prominent Americans. On November 12 ,1915, through the industrialist Robert Wooley, he met Col. Edward M. House, confidant, adviser, and close personal friend of Woodrow Wilson. The colonel, who until then "had an idea that Paderewski was an egoist of the most violent and offensive type," was, by the end of their first meeting, impressed by his charm and flattery. "He did not indicate," House recorded in his diary, "a trace of such characteristics in his interview with me." Paderewski told House of the destitution of the Polish people and of his inability to raise sufficient relief funds in America. Consequently he wanted House to persuade the United States Government to take some kind of official action in behalf of the Polish population in Europe. Paderewski's "sorrowful tale of the woes of Poland" deeply moved the colonel. At the end of their interview he promised the grateful Paderewski "to think the matter over and to see him again on Thursday of next week." [1] Not long afterward Paderewski became the "colonel's pet." [2]

The day after this first meeting House approached the British ambassador and asked if he could suggest any way to relieve the distress in Poland. The ambassador "ambled along for quite a while, telling what might be done in a diplomatic way, which summed up was nothing at all, excepting to say to the German officials that we [the United States] disapproved of what was being done in Poland, but they must not take what we [the United States] said as anything but an unofficial and private opinion of their actions." [3]

A few days later House began to interest Wilson in the Polish relief question, and from then on, whenever an opportunity arose,

1. House diary, Nov. 12, 1915. According to Landau, Paderewski first met House on Mar. 10, 1916; this is an error. Landau, *Paderewski,* p. 114.
2. Stephen Bonsal, *Unfinished Business* (New York, Doubleday, Doran, 1944), p. 76. "House was attracted by Paderewski's charm. The brilliant and enthusiastic Pole," Landau wrote, "contrasted so strikingly with the silent matter-of-fact House that the latter enjoyed the acquaintance of Paderewski as something unusual and entertaining." Landau, *Paderewski,* p. 114.
3. House diary, Nov. 13, 1915.

he reminded the president of the matter.[4] When Paderewski came to see House on November 18, House told him what he had done since they last met and promised not to slacken his efforts for Poland until he was either successful or could do no more. Paderewski, hearing this, broke down, took House's hands in his, and with tears in his eyes said "God bless you." [5]

When Mayor Newton Baker of Cleveland came to House to discuss with him a project that Baker had set on foot to raise more than $100,000,000 for the poor of Europe at the end of the war, the colonel immediately saw a further opportunity to help Paderewski. "I took this occasion," House recalled, "to explain the conditions of stricken Poland. I drew as graphic a picture of the misfortunes of that unhappy people as I could. I made him [Baker] feel that Belgium, where so much money had been donated, was a garden spot in comparison, and I urged him to form a committee and to raise this large sum now and not to wait until the war was ended, but give the people of Poland a helping hand." The mayor promised to undertake the work at once and to keep the colonel informed of progress. House in turn promised to try to iron out any diplomatic difficulties that might arise. Significantly enough, at the end of their discussion House asked Baker "if he thought himself a suitable man for National Chairman . . . [or] may be [sic] governor of Ohio." Baker refused both offers.[6]

The next time Paderewski saw House was on December 21, 1915. The pianist wished to thank the colonel for his services to Poland, particularly for the president's proclamation setting aside New Year's Day for contributions to Polish relief.[7] He objected only to the fund's being disbursed by the Red Cross. Food and politics have an inevitable and inseparable connection during wars; that Paderewski knew. His power and prestige among the American Poles depended on his control of food distribution and the large relief funds. He asked that the Polish National Committee be allowed to undertake the distribution of the relief—and not long afterward gained his wish.

That same December 21 Paderewski wrote House a flattering letter which according to the colonel was "one of the most delightful" he had received in a long time. "Words cannot express what I

4. *Ibid.,* Nov. 28, 1915.
5. *Ibid.,* Nov. 18, 1915.
6. *Ibid.,* Dec. 3, 1915.
7. *Ibid.,* Dec. 21, 1915.

feel for you," it read in part. "It has been the dream of my life to find a providential man for my country. I am now sure that I have not been dreaming vain dreams, because I had the happiness at meeting you. . . ." [8]

Within a few months the friendship bore fruit. House gave Paderewski access to the president of the United States.[9] In the summer of 1916,[10] upon House's recommendation, Paderewski was invited to dinner at the White House, where he entertained the host and his guests with the music of Chopin. After the playing, Landau recalled, Poland was the only subject of conversation.[11] Paderewski reminded Wilson of the "crime of partitions" and told him that all the Poles in America would support him in the coming election.[12] "Wilson's keen sense of justice and the rights of men," Landau declared, "was deeply shocked by the historic crime committed on the Polish nation. It was the sort of cause that appealed to him: its political aspect was for him less important than the larger moral issue. The idea of the rehabilitation of Poland had acquired the attraction of a moral task. . . . One could reasonably expect the seed which Paderewski had planted to grow in that heavy but fertile soil." [13]

Paderewski next met Wilson on November 6, 1916. That was the day of the presidential election, and Wilson, who retired to Shadow Lawn to await the results, asked Paderewski "to come to see him in order to thank him for his support in the election campaign." [14]

After the preliminary greetings the conversation between the two turned to Poland. According to Paderewski's official biographer, the president after shaking hands asked: " 'What do you think of the German manifesto?' [15] Paderewski told him that he

8. Paderewski to House, Dec. 22, 1915, House MSS.

9. Aniela Strakacz, *Paderewski as I Knew Him* (New Brunswick, N.J., Rutgers University Press, 1949), p. 134.

10. It has been impossible to fix an exact date. There is no mention in the House diary or in the Wilson papers. Landau only mentions "summer of 1916," but since he has proven to be inaccurate about dates, it is possible that the dinner may have occurred on Mar. 7, 1916. In the House diary we find this entry for the above date: "There was a large musicale given at the White House tonight."

11. See the complete description of the "party" in Landau, *Paderewski*, p. 113, and also in Smogorzewski, *Poland's Access to the Sea*, p. 91.

12. Marjan Seyda, *Polska, 1*, 483–4.

13. Landau, *Paderewski*, p. 113.

14. *Ibid.*, p. 115.

15. *Ibid.*, In the manifesto Germany and Austria-Hungary declared their willingness to establish a Polish kingdom.

took the manifesto to mean a German desire for more troops, and that he thought that it would result in a State without real freedom, dependent upon Germany." Wilson is said to have replied: "I am glad to see that we both absolutely agree about the subject." [16] It was before Paderewski took his leave, that Wilson added "in that slow, grave manner which so often gave his utterances the weight and solemnity of a nonconformist sermon: 'My dear Paderewski, I can tell that Poland will be resurrected and will exist again. For Poland this miracle of independence will come from the West, as my own victory will come through a miracle from the West.' " [17]

After Wilson's electoral victory his interest in Poland diminished. He became vitally absorbed in the issues involving the renewal of submarine warfare and in the attempts to interest the Allies in a mediated peace. The official policy of the United States toward the Polish problem remained unchanged. Most of Wilson's personal advisers were pro-Polish and in a short time steered him to a Polish policy about which he had some misgivings. His most important adviser, Colonel House, was by his own admission a sincere friend of Poland and pushed her fortunes at every possible opportunity.[18] "It was solely through Paderewski," House recorded, "that I became so deeply interested in the cause of Poland, and repeatedly passed upon the President Paderewski's views which I had made my own. That was the real influence that counted. . . ." [19]

The most dramatic meeting between Paderewski and Colonel House, according to Landau and Smogorzewski, occurred on January 8, 1917.[20] On that day Paderewski visited House who, in the course of the interview, asked him to prepare as soon as possible a detailed memorandum on the Polish problem.[21] The president,

16. *Ibid.*
17. *Ibid.*
18. House diary, Jan. 17, 1917.
19. House to Orlowski, Jan. 15, 1931, House MSS.
20. House diary, Jan. 8, 1917.
21. According to Landau it was House who visited Paderewski. But in his diary for Jan. 8 House wrote: "Paderewski followed Mrs. Pringsheim. He wished to explain the trouble which would probably follow the coming of the new Austrian Ambassador Tarnowski. The Austrian Poles plan to give him a great welcome which Paderewski thinks will be resented by the Poles in general, and that all sorts of complications may ensue. He thought the proposals of a new Poland made by Russia and Germany were absolutely selfish. Germany proposes to take a part of Russian Poland in order to strengthen her eastern frontier, while Russia wants to create a Poland composed of Russian, German and Austrian Poland for the purposes of securing Dantzig for a Russian port." Paderewski did give House some memoranda regarding Poland. House's diary for Jan. 17 reads: "Paderewski called to make some corrections in the memoranda he gave me the other day. . . ."

WILSON, HOUSE, AND PADEREWSKI   71

House said, was preparing a very important international statement. The colonel himself was leaving in a few days' time to see him
in Washington. Paderewski shut himself up and worked for
"thirty-six hours on end." When House left New York on the 11th
he carried in his pocket "the detailed exposé dealing with the necessity for an independent Poland." [22] House returned from
Washington several days later. When Paderewski asked him about
his memorandum, House answered:

> Yes, certainly. *En route* to Washington I read your text four
> or five times. I learned by heart the essential passages. During
> the following days, when lunching and dining with the Presi-
> dent, I continuously brought forward your arguments. In sev-
> eral cases he declared himself absolutely in agreement with
> your propositions. To-day he has shut himself up to prepare
> his message in solitude. The bomb will go off in a few days. It
> will take your breath away. . . .[23]

On January 22, 1917, Wilson—in his famous "peace without
victory" speech—for the first time in his capacity as president of
the United States spoke of the future of Poland. "Statesmen
everywhere," he said, "are agreed that there should be a united,
independent and autonomous Poland." [24]

The seed planted almost two years earlier in the president's
mind seemed to have grown to full maturity. Wilson's assertion
about "statesmen everywhere" cannot, however, be taken as proof
of his pro-Polish policy or as a factor leading to the re-establishment of Poland. It in no way involved or indicated the course of
American foreign policy in regard to Poland. Far from being a
lecture to the belligerent powers, the statement was simply a reit-
eration of a fact already in existence. For, as we know, both the
Central Powers and Russia had by that time already promised an
autonomous Poland. House himself admits this. After reviewing
with the president the draft of the January 22 speech, House
wrote: "We thought that since Germany and Russia had agreed
to free Poland that should be put in. We naturally agreed upon
Belgium and Serbia being restored, Alsace and Lorraine we were
not quite certain of, but we agreed that Turkey should cease to

22. Landau, *Paderewski*, p. 118.
23. Smogorzewski, *Poland's Access to the Sea*, p. 92. For a similar version of
this see Landau, *Paderewski*, p. 118. The probable date of this statement is January 17, 1917, when Paderewski called on House to express his appreciation for
House's efforts in behalf of Poland.
24. For the complete text see Filasiewicz, *La Question polonaise*, p. 134.

exist. . . ." [25] Nevertheless this statement of January 22, whether because of its ambiguity or its ostensible hidden meaning, won the president the friendship of many Poles in America and gave him a prominent place in Polish history.

The governments of the partitioning powers, as well as France and Great Britain, were unfavorably impressed. Once again the Polish question was opened. Berlin suspected that Wilson was proposing to rob Germany of her Polish territories in the peace settlement. The tsarist government immediately started negotiations with France and finally agreed with the latter (11 March 1917) that, in return for recognizing her claims to Alsace-Lorraine and right to fix the eastern frontier, Russia should receive the right to determine her own western limit, that is, to include as much of Poland as she could reconquer.[26] This agreement, one of the last acts of tsarist Russia, did not survive the revolution of 1917.

The entrance of America into the war put a new aspect on relations with the Allies concerning Poland. Hitherto the United States had been the leading neutral power to champion the Polish cause. Now it became an active participant and, as such, was able to exert greater influence in behalf of Wilsonian ideals for a new order in the world.

The belligerent status of the United States also increased the

25. House diary, Jan. 3, 1917. Compare this succinct statement with House's flowery remarks to Paderewski on Jan. 17(?). See above, pp. 70–1. It is also important to remember that it was only after President Wilson requested the belligerent powers to define their general war aims that the Western Allies for the first time stated formally, but still ambiguously, their attitude toward Poland. In their answer to Wilson's request of Dec. 18, 1916, they declared that victory should bring the restitution of provinces formerly torn from the Allies by force or against the wish of their inhabitants, the liberation of the Italians, as also of the Slavs, Rumanians, and Czecho-Slovaks from foreign domination, and the expulsion from Europe of the Ottoman Empire. This statement did not include Poland at all, but the public-at-large believed that the term "Slavs" meant the Poles. See H. W. V. Temperley, *History of the Peace Conference* (London, Frowle, 1921), *1, 172.* Wilson also was convinced that the proclamation clearly and justly indicated a true and fair policy! See Filasiewicz, *La Question polonaise,* p. 122.

26. Russian ambassador in Paris (Izwolski) to Minister of Foreign Affairs Pokrowski, Mar. 11, 1917, Filasiewicz, *La Question polonaise,* p. 140. Izwolski's confidential telegram read: "Le gouvernement de la République française, soucieux de confirmer toute l'importance et la signification des accords conclus avec le gouvernement russe, en 1916, à l'effet de régler, à la fin de la guerre actuelle, la question de Constantinople et des Détroits d'une façon conforme aux aspirations de la Russie; soucieux, d'autre part, d'assurer à son alliée, tant au point de vue militaire qu'au point de vue industriel, toutes les garanties désirables pour la sécurité et le développement économique de l'Empire, reconnaî à la Russie la complète liberté de déterminer à son gré ses frontières occidentales." See also Harold Nicolson, *Peacemaking, 1919* (Boston and New York, 1933), p. 139.

power and prestige of Colonel House, the avowed friend of Poland. Realizing that the president's address of January 22 had adversely impressed Great Britain, House took it upon himself to influence that government. His conversation with Balfour on April 28, 1917, clearly reveals his intent. President Wilson, not wishing to know "formally" about the secret treaties of the Allies, asked House to meet the British statesman informally.[27] Here is House's record of the important conversation:

> He [Balfour] first discussed Poland and outlined what its boundaries should be. Of course, the stumbling block was the outlet to the sea. There can be no other excepting Danzig. . . . Balfour thought it might be made a free port, and in this way satisfy Poland. At that moment, I do not look upon this with favor, particularly since the Germans and Poles would be antagonistic and ready upon the slightest provocation to find grievances against one another. However, I warmly advocated a restored and rejuvenated Poland, a Poland big enough and powerful enough to serve as a buffer state between Germany and Russia. . . . His objection to a Polish state, cutting off Russia from Germany, was whether it would not hurt France more than Germany, for the reason it would prevent Russia from coming to France's aid in the event of an attack under Germany. *I thought we had to take under consideration the Russia of fifty years from now rather than the Russia of to-day.* . . . Balfour, however, was more impressed with the German menace than he was by the possible danger from Russia.[28]

The colonel's attempt to influence Balfour was not as successful as Paderewski's efforts to influence House and Wilson had been. A few weeks after their meeting Balfour, at a secret session of the British Imperial War Council, was obliged to state Great Britain's

27. According to Baker, Colonel House and Balfour conferred on Apr. 28, 1917, for an hour and a half, at the president's request, on the subject of peace terms. On Jan. 13, 1922, House informed Baker that Balfour "explained" to him the secret treaties that the Allies had made during the war. Balfour, House wrote in his letter to Baker, "did not have copies of the secret treaties with him, but I suggested it would be well to have them sent for the information of the President and the State Department. Whether this was done I do not know, but Mr. Balfour was entirely frank in discussing the treaties and showed no inclination whatever to conceal any of the facts. . . ." Baker, *Woodrow Wilson, 7,* 40, 40n., 74, 75.

28. Charles Seymour, ed., *The Intimate Papers of Colonel House* (4 vols. New York, Houghton-Mifflin, 1926–28), *3,* 43–6 (italics inserted).

attitude toward Poland. He reviewed briefly the history of Poland
and the means of getting rid of the "crime of the Polish partitions." It was true, he said, that Poland had brought disaster
upon herself:

> If Poland had understood the elements of reasonably good gov-
> ernment, the idea that she could be partitioned like an inert
> mass, as she was, is out of the question. But that is the past,
> and it is quite possible that the Poland of the future will be a
> useful member of the European community; but until she is
> satisfied you will have this nucleus of bitter discontent, and a
> nation going back to great and glorious memories, when it was
> the most powerful state in Eastern Europe.[29]

He told the members of the council that Roman Dmowski had
urged in the strongest terms making a public appeal on behalf of
Poland. Now that the tsar had gone, the Polish leader had argued,
the Entente ought to announce publicly that they were going to
establish an independent Poland; otherwise there would be great
danger of the Germans succeeding in future in doing what they
had failed to do in the past: raising a Polish army. "I put this
question to him," Balfour continued: "the Tsar has gone, and with
the Tsar an obstacle may have gone, but can you ask this new
Russian Government to begin its career by handing over what the
Russians regard as an indisputable part of their territory?" [30]

Dmowski thought he could, but Balfour had his doubts. In
concluding the British statesman made this important statement:

> Personally, from a selfish Western point of view, I would rather
> that Poland was autonomous under the Russians, because if
> you make an absolutely independent Poland lying between
> Russia and the Central States, you cut off Russia altogether
> from the West. Russia ceases to be a factor in Western politics,
> or almost ceases. She will be largely divided from Germany by
> the new Polish State; and she will not be coterminous with any
> of the belligerents. And if Germany has designs in the future
> upon France or the West, I think she will be protected by this
> new State from any action on the part of Russia, and I am not
> at all sure that that is to the interests of Western civiliza-
> tion. . . .[31]

29. Balfour to Secretary of State, May 18, 1917, *FR: Lansing Papers, 2,* 27.
30. *Ibid.,* 29.
31. *Ibid.,* 28.

Within a few months after President Wilson's declaration on behalf of Poland, Paderewski, certain now that Colonel House was his "providential man," [32] began to press his friend to allow him to organize a unit of Poles in the army of the United States. At first he presented to House no more than an offer from the pro-Paderewski Polish societies in America to furnish five hundred trained officers in the event of war. The training of these officers was to be without cost to the government.[33] House showed interest and asked Paderewski to supply him with additional data about the offer. The next day his request was answered.[34]

Certain of Wilson's acquiescence, once House had shown approval, Paderewski began to make the necessary arrangements for recruiting Polish officers in America.[35] When weeks passed without any official word from the president, Paderewski became worried. On March 10, 1917, he called on House to find out whether anything could be done to get Wilson's permission. Again House promised to help him. The next day the colonel wrote the following letter to Wilson:

> Paderewski called yesterday to say that his patriots are anxious to know your decision regarding their offer. They have gone to considerable expense already in the renting of houses and a hotel at the place where they expect to undertake the training of the five hundred officers.
>
> Paderewski told me at one time that at least fifty thousand Poles would enlist for service if called for.
>
> I explained to him that you had been ill and had not had time to take the matter up with the Secretary of War. . . .[36]

While waiting for an answer Paderewski began to cultivate House with renewed vigor. During their many lunches and suppers

32. On May 14 Paderewski gave House a photograph of himself with the following inscription: "To Colonel E. M. House, with expression of everlasting gratitude." In order to make House realize that he considered him responsible for Wilson's declaration for a reconstructed Poland he symbolically dated it Jan. 22, the day of the president's speech. House diary, May 14, 1917.

33. Several months later the societies asked the Government of the United States for $600,000 per month to cover this training. See Lansing to Wilson, Dec. 24, 1917, Wilson MSS. See also House diary, Feb. 27, 1917.

34. House diary, Feb. 28, 1917.

35. Throughout this period Polish Falcon organizations trained young Polish-Americans. When, one day, their guns were taken away from them, Paderewski rushed to House in great excitement, asking why. House immediately called Commissioner Woods and "peace soon reigned in Polish quarters." *Ibid.,* Apr. 11, 1917.

36. House to Wilson, Mar. 11, 1917, House MSS.

Paderewski "saturated" House with facts concerning the Polish problem.[37] At one of their meetings House became somewhat suspicious of Paderewski's presumptuous statements and told him that he did not wish to be misled in any way concerning Poland because he always desired to be accurate in any statement he made. Paderewski said nothing at the time. But the captivating artist contrived to lull House's suspicion. At a recital shortly afterward the colonel noticed that Paderewski played with unusual fervor. "I had never heard such music," House recorded, "and I was lifted out of myself. . . . I sat in a box just above him and he continuously looked into my face as he played. I felt at the time he was trying to please me. . . ." When they met again and House congratulated him on his splendid performance, Paderewski said that he had "poured out his soul" to him, for he was deeply hurt that House had doubted his sincerity. "I come to you," the pianist declared, "as I would to my God without holding back anything." That day House wrote in his diary: "Paderewski is an emotional soul, and I am as tender in my treatment of him as I would be of a highly sensitive child." [38]

Shortly afterward Paderewski, now fully convinced that through House he had won Wilson to his side, wrote to Secretary Newton D. Baker asking him to give permission to organize a unit of Poles in the army of the United States. When Baker forwarded this request to the president for his consideration, Wilson answered: "This is a most interesting proposition but I think your own reflections upon it are very wise and that it would be a mistake, at any rate at this stage of our own preparation, to organize a force of the sort proposed. I agree with you that there are many advantages in this plan and many striking and impressive things about it, but this is not the stage at which to act upon the suggestion. We must keep this in store for later action." [39]

Wilson's refusal came as a shock to the overconfident Paderewski. But it did not stop him. He found a willing listener in Secretary of State Robert Lansing. The latter, like House at first adversely impressed by Paderewski, was won over by the Pole's

37. House diary, Mar. 2, 4 and Apr. 11, 19, 1917.
38. *Ibid.*, May 14, 1917.
39. On the same day, May 21, 1917, Wilson saw Balfour. "While no record exists of this interview," Baker wrote, "it is practically certain that the subject matter had to do with secret treaties." Baker, *Woodrow Wilson,* p. 80n. If Baker is correct in the above statement it is likely that the subject of Poland was touched upon in the conversation.

earnestness and charm. On June 12, 1917, Lansing informed Wilson that he had been turning over in his mind

> in what way we can best utilize the intense longing of the Poles for the restoration of Poland as an independent nation. It seems to be recognized by all the Allies that Polish independence should be one of the results of the war and that the Poles should as far as possible be segregated into military units so that they would feel their nationality and be inspired to fight for the freedom of their country.[40]

In the same letter he told the president of his understanding that France had already taken steps to form a skeleton on which to build up a Polish army to fight on the western front; something of a like nature, he suggested, could be organized on the eastern front. To gain the full benefit of the Poles' loyalty to their country, Lansing said, the governments of the United States and of the Allies should

> announce in separate but identical declarations that they recognize the legitimate nature of Polish desire for self-government and they propose to devote their energies to free Poland and restore the nation to full sovereignty, in contradistinction to a nation under the protection or control of any neighboring power.[41]

Lansing further proposed that America should finance the Polish military establishment.

> My suggestion is that a Polish Provisional Government [be] set up in this country, that it be recognized by this Government and the Allied Governments, and that it send diplomatic representatives to all the powers . . . After formal recognition of this Government of an independent Poland we could legally loan the Government for military purposes the necessary funds secured by Polish bonds underwritten by this country and the Allies.[42]

After careful consideration, the secretary of state wrote, and in order to avoid all suspicion "as to the genuine purpose of this step looking to the rebirth of Poland this country is the only place.

40. Lansing, *The Big Four,* pp. 201–3.
41. Lansing to Wilson, June 21, 1917, *FR: Lansing Papers, 2,* 35–6.
42. *Ibid.*

Furthermore . . . the new Government should be where we can keep a watchful eye on the expenditures." [43] If this plan, Lansing concluded, "or one along the same lines meets your approval, shall I sound the diplomatic representatives of the Allies on the subject?" [44]

There was no need for Lansing to ask Wilson's permission to sound the diplomatic representatives of the Allies. In the summer of 1917, when the disintegration of the Russian armies could no longer be ignored and the fear that the Germans and Austrians might use Polish troops became a reality, the British Foreign Office began to make overtures to the United States Government. On July 23, 1917, the British Embassy in Washington informed the secretary of state that His Majesty's Government was much concerned over the enemy's "specious assurances of a spurious independence to the Polish people." British Intelligence learned that the Poles felt themselves abandoned by the Allies, and hence the assurances of the enemy were welcome.[45] "In consequence," the British ambassador wrote, "His Majesty's Government propose that all Poles, whether of German, Austrian or Prussian origin, living in the countries of the Allied powers should be granted open recognition as friends and potential allies." As a corollary to such action the British Foreign Office felt that a committee should be established to represent the Polish community in each of the Allied countries.[46]

On August 27, 1917, Lansing, having in all probability received Wilson's permission to approach the diplomatic representatives of the Allied Powers about Poland, sent a telegram to the American ambassador in Great Britain informing him that his department had been considering the establishment of a provisional Polish government. Upon recognition, Lansing advised him, it would be possible to recruit Poles residing in the United States, either above or below the draft age if they were naturalized Americans, and of any age if aliens. The army so recruited was to be trained in Canada and later moved to Europe on English transports. It was to be commanded by an American or Polish general

43. *Ibid.*
44. *Ibid.*
45. It is quite possible that the British Intelligence had also learned that Germany and Austria were about to establish a council of regency for the Polish kingdom. They did so on September 12, 1917.
46. British Embassy to Department of State, July 23, 1917, *FR: 1917,* Supplement 2, *1,* 759–60.

under either the American or Polish flag and to fight in conjunction with American troops in France. "You are requested informally and orally," Lansing wrote to Page, "to sound the British Government, ascertaining whether the present time is considered opportune for action as above suggested." [47]

As the pressure from the United States increased, the Polish question assumed greater importance in Great Britain. There, as well as in the United States, the naturalized Poles and their sympathizers were strongly organized. Soon the British Government became concerned over the Polish vote [48] in Great Britain as well as over the military catastrophies on the Russian front. On September 3, 1917, the British Foreign Office sent Sir William Wiseman to the United States to act as liaison between the British Government and Wilson and House. One of his responsibilities was to study the Polish problem in America. Before leaving Great Britain Wiseman sent the following cable to Colonel House: "The Polish question is assuming a growing importance. Unfortunately the Poles in America are divided. . . . I am bringing with me the fullest information we possess regarding this question and suggest any decision of policy by the United States Government should be held up until I place our information before you." [49]

Immediately upon his arrival in the United States Sir William Wiseman entered into long conversations with Colonel House. As soon as Paderewski learned of Wiseman's mission (in all probability from Jan Horodyski, a British Pole who accompanied Wiseman) [50] he hurried to see his old friend House. Fully briefed on the latest American démarche and the British conversion to the Polish cause, Paderewski amid extravagant gratitude and praise urged House to hasten the establishment and recognition of a provisional government of Poland. He spoke of House as having been sent by God to deliver Poland and said he saw House's hand "everywhere and always helping Poland." He attributed the British conversion to the Polish cause to House. "There is some truth in this last," the colonel recorded, "and more in the credit he gives me for what the

47. Secretary of State to the Ambassador in Great Britain (Page), Aug. 27, 1917, *ibid.*, pp. 760–61. The British reply to Page's subsequent inquiry stated that although Lord Robert Cecil heartily agreed "in spirit" he did not wish to commit himself at that particular time, but that he would welcome further information in this matter. Page to Secretary of State, Sept. 4, 1917, *ibid.*, p. 752.

48. Wiseman to Drummond, Oct. 9, 1917, House MSS.

49. Wiseman to House, Sept. 3, 1917, House MSS.

50. See Wiseman to Drummond, Oct. 9, 1917, House MSS.

President has said in behalf of Poland." Paderewski also told House that he was the only man since Napoleon I who had understood the importance of a reconstructed Poland to the peace of Europe. These statements left House "dumb with confusion. If he were less *naive* and childlike," House recorded in his diary, "I would be suspicious of him." [51]

Several days later Paderewski telegraphed President Wilson at length, informing him that a Polish National Department had recently been established in Chicago—a federation of all important Polish organizations in the United States "representing an overwhelming majority, approximately 90 per cent of Polish people living in this country." [sic] . . . a great many of these people are loyal citizens of the United States. . . . Out of the four millions of them not one is a millionaire." The telegram mentioned that the French Government, because of political and strategic need to check the designs of the enemy, had decided to form a national Polish army on the western front; and referred to the United States Government's decision not to object to recruiting Polish volunteers in this country. Furthermore both British and French Governments, Paderewski stated, in order to put an end to pro-German intrigue had agreed to recognize the Polish National Committee formed in Paris [52] "as official experts on Polish questions and unofficial representatives of the Polish nation provided that the United States Government would recognize it as well." [53]

The telegram ended with a moving plea to Wilson to recognize the Polish National Committee in Paris as the official spokesman for the Polish people:

51. House diary, Sept. 22, 1917.

52. The officers of the committee at Paris were Roman Dmowski, president; Erasme Piltz, Jan J. Rozwadowski, Marjan Seyda, Count Maurice Zamoyski, I. J. Paderewski, representing America; Count Ladislas Sobanski, representing Great Britain; Count Constantine Skirmunt, representative to Italy. All of them were either National Democrats or Realists.

53. Even before this telegram was sent the Polish National Department of "loyal citizens of the United States" agreed to unite with the Paris Committee headed by foreigners! On Oct. 3 this Polish National Department sent the following message to the Polish National Committee in Paris: "Conscious of the importance of our act and the solemnity of the occasion, we have this day unanimously agreed to unite with the National Polish Committee in Paris. We welcome with joy our representation on this committee in the person of Ignace Jan Paderewski. We pledge our loyal cooperation and acknowledge the political supremacy of your committee. At the same time we desire to express our conviction that your committee should embrace representatives of as many Polish political parties as possible, in order to strengthen its authority. . . ." *FR: 1917*, Supplement 2, *1*, 763–4.

Mr. President, the issue of this gigantic struggle between light and darkness, between right and brutal power depends on you. The fate of peoples and governments is in your hands. The wealth and might of this huge Republic made you the principal leader of consolidated human efforts; the greatness and generosity of your character made you the supreme commander of God's forces. You are the foster-father of a chiefless land. You are Poland's inspired protector. For many a month the spelling of your name has been the only comfort and joy of a starving nation. For many a month among the ruins of a devastated country millions of people have been feeding on you.

Now on the 14th of October the bells of Polish churches, of those still remaining, will call upon the faithful to join in fervent prayer in memory of the noble hero departed a hundred years ago, Thaddeus Kosciuszko. If on that day the news could reach the country that the Polish National Committee in Paris has been recognized, the Polish national army has been sanctioned by our beloved President Wilson, this would certainly give new strength, new hope and new courage to the stricken nation which trusts but God and you.

"This is the object my people entrusted me to most respectfully lay before you, together with their unanimous offering of veneration and everlasting gratitude.[54]

It is significant to note that a few days later, October 8, 1917, the War Department made a public announcement allowing American Poles, not subject to the draft, to enlist in the Polish Army recruited in the United States.[55] On October 12 recruiting began. Within the same week the State Department undertook arrangements to recognize the Paris Committee.[56] The only obstacle to America's early recognition was Russia. The Russian Foreign Office refused to allow the Poles to establish a separate army for fear the Central Powers would immediately call up the Poles within their jurisdiction and thus increase their force by 800,000 men.[57] Not until three days after the Bolshevik Revolution of November 7, 1917, did the United States recognize the Polish National Committee in Paris as an official organization.[58] A year later,

54. Paderewski to Wilson, Oct. 4, 1917, *FR : 1917,* Supplement 2, *1,* 762–4.
55. *Ibid.,* p. 765.
56. For the correspondence dealing with the above see *ibid.,* pp. 765–90.
57. Francis to Secretary of State, Oct. 22, 1917, *ibid.,* pp. 776–7.
58. Secretary of State to Sharp, Nov. 10, 1917, *ibid.,* p. 778.

on November 1, 1918, the Polish Army, "under the supreme political authority of the Polish National Committee," was recognized by the United States as autonomous and cobelligerent.[59]

The Bolshevik Revolution and especially the negotiations at Brest-Litovsk forced Wilson to take a personal hand in the Polish problem. Soviet propaganda emanating from Brest-Litovsk, where the Soviets promised independence to the Poles and other nationalities, had to be countered by the Allies.[60] In a declaration of British War and Peace Conditions, Lloyd George, on January 5, 1918, said: "The consent of the governed must be the basis of any territorial settlement. . . ."[61] This declaration, the prime minister stated, inferentially included Poland.[62] But it fell to Wilson to answer Soviet propaganda fully.[63] Three days later he announced his Fourteen Points, the thirteenth of which dealt exclusively with Poland.

The thirteenth point was the result of the recommendation of "The Inquiry" and Paderewski's influence on House. In the summer of 1917 Colonel House, foreseeing the need of careful research and planning to guide the American delegation at a future peace conference, suggested to Wilson that a commission of investigation be established. The president agreed, and an organization called the Inquiry, under the direction of Dr. Mezes, was created. A staff of over 150 historians and specialists, including such men as Walter Lippmann, Dr. Isaiah Bowman, David Hunter Miller, and Professor J. T. Shotwell, compiled statistics, wrote memoranda, and drew maps.[64] Within the Inquiry there was a Polish committee presided over by Robert H. Lord, then professor at Harvard. As collaborators he had two Poles, Professors Arctowski and Zwierzchowski (Zowski).[65]

On December 22, 1917, almost three weeks before the announcement of the Fourteen Points, the Inquiry finished its study of the Polish problem. Its memorandum (Inquiry Document No.

59. *Ibid., 1918,* Supplement 1, *1,* 880–1.
60. Marjan Seyda, *Polska, 1,* 434–5. See also Hajo Holborn, *The Political Collapse of Europe* (New York, 1951), p. 90.
61. David Lloyd George, *Memoirs of the Peace Conference* (New Haven, Yale University Press, 1939), *2,* 630–1.
62. *Ibid.*
63. Holborn, *The Political Collapse of Europe,* p. 90.
64. Seymour, *Intimate Papers, 3,* 171.
65. *FR: Paris Peace Conference, 1919, 1,* 87–8. In all probability Professor Zwierzchowski anglicized his name to Zowski. See Roman Dmowski, *Polityka Polska,* p. 392.

887) categorically stated: "An independent and democratic Poland shall be established. Its boundaries shall be based on a fair balance of national and economic considerations, giving full weight the necessity for adequate access to the sea. The form of Poland's government and its economic and political relations should be left to the determination of the people of Poland acting through their chosen representatives." [66]

In the final drafting of the thirteenth point Colonel House was also guided by a memorandum which the Polish National Committee in Paris sent him. This memorandum included a paragraph which the committee wished the Interallied Conference to incorporate in its war aims: "The reconstitution of an independent Polish state comprising Polish territories which before the war belonged to Russia, Germany and Austria. This Polish state to be in possession of the Polish part of Silesia and a part of the Baltic coast with the mouths of the Vistula and the Niemen; to have proper extension and a sufficiently large population to enable it to become an efficient factor of European equilibrium." [67]

House presented this memorandum to Wilson during their discussion of Poland. Both of them read it over carefully, and although they felt that the memorandum could not be used in full, the paragraph which they eventually framed "came as near to it," House recorded, "as we felt was wise and expedient": [68] "An independent Polish state should be erected, which should include the territories inhabited by indisputably Polish populations, which should be assured a free and secure access to the sea, and whose political and economic independence and territorial integrity, should be guaranteed by international covenant." [69]

None of the phrases, be it noted, was precise. Only the last

66. FR: Paris Peace Conference, 1919, 1, 51-2.

67. Dmowski to Sharp, Nov. 13, 1917, FR: 1917, Supplement 2, 1, 789.

68. House's account of the conversation with Wilson regarding the drafting of the Fourteen Points reads as follows: "He spent some time on Poland. I gave him the memoranda which the Polish National Council in Paris had given me, containing a paragraph which they wished the Interallied Conference to adopt, but which was refused. We read this over carefully and both concluded that it could not be used in full, but the paragraph as framed came as near to it as he felt was wise and expedient." Seymour, Intimate Papers, 3, 332.

69. It is interesting to note that the last phrase of the Polish prototype of the thirteenth point, which envisaged a return to balance-of-power politics in Europe, was completely changed by Wilson. Instead the president, who disliked any reference to balance of power, gave the future League of Nations the power to guarantee the political and economic independence and territorial integrity of Poland. FR: 1918, Supplement 1, 1, 16.

approached the specific in that it left the future League of Nations to deal with the "political and economic" integrity of Poland. What did Wilson mean by "territories inhabited by indisputably Polish populations?" What did he mean by assuring "a free and secure access to the sea?" Was there any significance in Wilson's use in the thirteenth point of the word "should," whereas when he dealt with the problem of Belgium, for example, he said "must"? According to House, Wilson and he agreed that where there was no difference of opinion as to the justice of a question the word "must" was used, and where there was a controversy the word "should" was used. "He [Wilson] went through the entire message," House recalled, "and corrected it in this way. He wondered whether that point would be caught. I thought it was certain it would be." [70] But nobody questioned the ambiguity or hidden meanings of the thirteenth point immediately.[71] Only when the Germans accepted the Fourteen Points as a basis for armistice did it become important and consequently more thoroughly analyzed.

The declaration of the Fourteen Points greatly influenced the Polish problem.[72] Point thirteen especially affected the situation within occupied Poland and, what is more important, increased Polish-American political pressure for early recognition of Polish independence. "It was not until then," according to Colonel House,

> that the German Poles, the Russian Poles, and the Austrian Poles felt the urge for united action, since President Wilson's call for justice for this ancient people sent a thrill through every Polish heart. Until then Poles in Central Empires had been fighting their kinsmen in Russia. In all three Empires sons of this proud and valiant nation were bound to the war

70. House diary, Jan. 9, 1918.

71. The possible exception was Paderewski. In his diary House records: "Paderewski came almost directly after our conference was over. . . . He was somewhat worried that the word 'should' was applied to Poland while 'must' was used for Belgium. I satisfied him on this point by telling him that it would not do to make an issue in the United States of the restoration of Poland as an ultimatum. He seemed to understand and assented." *Ibid.*, Jan. 12, 1918.

72. After the declaration of the Fourteen Points Paderewski came to see House. "Paderewski," House wrote, "came almost directly. . . . He expressed himself in such an extravagant way that I always hesitate to repeat what he says, although I know he must say practically the same thing to the President. He greeted me as follows: 'I come to kneel at your feet. You are the noblest man I have ever had the honor to know. You stand by yourself, unapproachable by any means by which ordinary men are reached and influenced.'" *Ibid.*

machines of each and were giving their lives to forge new links in a chain which had galled them for centuries.[73]

In consequence of Wilson's Fourteen Points a great number of Poles in America and in Europe became pro-American and pro-Wilson. To many Americans President Wilson's foreign policy seemed general and idealistic, but to some Poles it was intensely actual and urgent.

73. House, "Paderewski: The Paradox of Europe," *Harper's Magazine 152* (1925), 30.

7. Wilson and Organized Polish-American Pressure

AFTER THE DECLARATION of the Fourteen Points it became necessary for Paderewski to organize the Poles in America under the leadership of the Polish National Committee in order to increase political pressure on the United States Government for early recognition of Polish independence. But this goal was not easy to achieve. As long as the Central Powers continued fighting, the pro-German and pro-Austrian Poles continued to support them.

Consequently the Polish National Committee at Paris and Paderewski, now its official representative in the United States, began to carry on extensive propaganda among the Polish-Americans, as well as among the Polish masses in the Allied countries and occupied Poland. Their endeavors, which involved considerable expenditures, were not at first successful. Most of the money for the propaganda to nullify the pro-German and pro-Austrian attitudes of the Poles came from Polish organizations in the United States and from the profits of the National Democratic party's newspapers and other enterprises in that part of Russian Poland not occupied by the enemy.

More money was needed; and what country could supply it but the rich and munificent United States? Paderewski approached Secretary of State Lansing, told him that the position of the committee at Paris was precarious because of lack of financial means, and asked whether the president or the Government of the United States would grant the following "trifling loan":

1. Sixty thousand dollars as a monthly subvention for the maintenance of agencies and offices already existing in Paris, London, Rome, Lausanne, and Petrograd as well as of those which are to be established in neutral countries, for the duration of the war.

2. One million dollars for the immediate relief of Polish refugees in Russia whose situation, under the present regime, is most critical and the number exceeds sixteen hundred thousand.

3. A subsidy of five hundred thousand dollars for the purpose of bringing over from Russia, five hundred experienced Polish officers of all ranks, already promised by the Russian

General Staff, and whose presence among the Polish soldiers would greatly increase the value of that fighting material.[1]

After receiving this request Lansing, on January 28, 1918, wrote the president recommending he advance from the president's war fund a minimum of $30,000 a month, with the proviso that the sum be placed under the control of an agent of the State Department to be attached to the American Embassy at Paris. He also suggested that the British Government should provide a like sum under the supervision of one of its own agents. "The understanding being," Lansing concluded, "that the Polish National Committee in return therefor will secure and place at the disposal of the British Government and this Government all information of a political and military character secured by its agents. . . ." The reason that Lansing did not advise the president to grant the total sum requested by the Poles was the Treasury's inability under law, to lend money except to established governments at war with the Central Powers.[2]

On January 29, Wilson replied to Lansing as follows:

I think I see this situation as a whole, and of course I am disposed to help in every way possible, but I do not feel at liberty to pledge thirty thousand dollars a month indefinitely. Would the Committee think it fair if I were to limit the pledge to (say) six months, pending developments?

And,—another question,—is it not likely that the portion to [the] British Government is to pay would in fact be drawn from our Treasury, by loan? I feel obliged to think of the financial burdens piling up on us.[3]

Wilson's reluctance to give even $30,000 a month for a minimum of six months out of the total requested did not arrest Paderewski's efforts to fatten the committee's treasury. Remembering Wilson's campaign speech of 1916, in which he failed to name a special day for Polish relief, Paderewski sent his wife to Wilson on February 27, 1918, to urge again [4] "that a day be set aside for

1. Paderewski to Lansing, Jan. 19, 1918, *FR: Lansing Papers, 2,* 71–3.
2. Lansing to Wilson, Jan. 28, 1918, *ibid.,* pp. 91–3.
3. Wilson to Lansing, Jan. 29, 1918, *ibid.,* p. 93. On Feb. 5 the British Government agreed to provide $30,000 a month for a minimum of six months provided the United States did the same. See Wiseman to Drummond, Feb. 5, 1918, House MSS.
4. See Edith Wilson, *My Memoir* (Indianapolis and New York, 1939), p. 113.

aid to the Polish people. . . ." [5] Wilson refused.[6] To him the Poles still remained "unorganized."

Again Wilson's refusal did not stop Paderewski. Since the only obstacle to the bestowal of the desired loan seemed to be the United States law which prevented granting such loans to unrecognized governments, he began to organize pressure among American Poles to influence American representatives and senators for early recognition of Polish independence.

As usual Paderewski first approached his friend the colonel. He asked House to use his personal influence to secure him the privilege of addressing the members of Congress in Washington.[7] House made the following notation on the letter: "P.[Paderewski] is eternally worked up about this. If the Secy can do anything with Flood [Congressman from Virginia of the House Committee on Foreign Affairs] or anyone else it would be wise to do so." The privilege was not obtained.

Paderewski succeeded in persuading Representative Gallagher to submit a bill for the recognition of Polish independence. The resolution was formulated as follows: ". . . the House of Representatives considers the creation of a free and independent Polish state, with access to the sea, to be one of the objects for which the United States is fighting in the present war, and as one of the necessary provisions in any treaty of peace which may be concluded." [8]

This bill was sent to President Wilson for his consideration before it was introduced in the House. Wilson immediately wrote Gallagher on his own typewriter, that this action was not wise. "If we are to be definite in the case of this particular national aspiration," Wilson wrote, "why not in the case of others, and where shall we stop, definition being at each step increasingly difficult." [9]

A few days later, on July 11, 1918, Wilson again received a contemplated bill for the recognition of Polish independence. This time the bill came from Senator G. M. Hitchcock. The president again replied by letter. He had talked with the secretary of state about the bill, he stated, and both agreed that in view of the numerous national groups in the United States the passage of a bill

5. Baker, *Woodrow Wilson, 7,* 568.
6. Wilson to Madame Paderewska, May 9, 1918, Wilson MSS.
7. Paderewski to House, May 24, 1918, House MSS.
8. Baker, *Woodrow Wilson, 8,* 267. See also Lansing to Wilson, June 14, 1918, *FR: Lansing Papers, 2,* 130.
9. Wilson to Gallagher, July 8, 1918, Baker, *Woodrow Wilson, 8, 267.*

taking all Poles out of the alien class would seriously embarrass the government.[10]

Wilson's negative answer did not prevent Senator Hitchcock from introducing the bill in the Senate. On July 18 the newspapers reported that a bill had been brought to the floor of the Senate by which the government was to recognize a free and independent Poland.[11] In the bill was a section requiring that the Polish National Committee in Paris be recognized as the official diplomatic representative of the new state and that its accredited representatives in America (that is Paderewski's group) should have the power to determine what persons among the nonnaturalized Poles should have the stigma of enemy aliens removed and who should not. American Poles who detested Paderewski denounced the bill immediately. They urged the Senate to reject the bill on the ground that it gave power to a committee which did not, according to them —and quite rightly—represent Poland.[12]

Opposition of many American Poles and Wilson's reluctance to recognize Polish independence forced Paderewski to more desperate action. He wrote to Roman Dmowski in Paris and asked him to come to the United States to help him organize the Polish-Americans.[13] Dmowski arrived in September 1918. He went immediately to Detroit to attend a congress of Poles. There by shrewd political maneuvers he and Paderewski succeeded in making the Paris Committee the sole controlling force in Polish affairs in America.

10. "While the passage of such a bill," Wilson wrote, "would take all the Poles out of the alien class under our existing statutes, it would involve this very serious embarrassment. The Czecho-Slovaks and the Jugo-Slavs have recently effected . . . an organization very similar to and quite as influential as the organization which the Poles have effected, and we are dealing with both. The Poles may be said to represent a definable territory, but the Czecho-Slovaks and the Jugo-Slavs do not. It is not likely that if they followed their own preferences, they would unite in a single state. I should not like in the present circumstances of unrest in the Austrian Empire to throw the least cold water upon the Bohemians and the Slavs to the south of them, and I fear separate action with regard to Poland would have that effect. . . ." Wilson to Hitchcock, July 13, 1918, *ibid., 8,* 275.

11. *New York Times,* July 18, 1918.

12. Jan Kobiet, "America and the Polish Question," *New Republic, 16* (1918), 44–6.

13. Paderewski was a faithful disciple of Dmowski. "Paderewski," wrote Landau, "had been very loyal to Dmowski during all this time. . . . During all the years of his political activity he had looked upon Dmowski as the legitimate head of the Polish affairs in the Western World, and no vital decision was reached, no change of policy accomplished, without an exchange of lengthy telegrams between the two men." Landau, *Paderewski,* p. 143.

At this Polish convention, ostensibly a representative body of American Poles, the affairs of Polish immigrants were given certain decisive, although dubious, settlements. Here Dmowski and Paderewski, armed with the prestige conferred upon them by the Allies, secured the support of the majority of the Polish organizations in America. In a speech opening the convention Paderewski stated: "The Poles in America do not need any Americanization." [14] Before the assembly adjourned a resolution passed which recognized the Paris Committee as controlling Polish affairs in America and abroad. This committed almost three million Americans to domination by a foreign group on foreign soil.

Many Poles at the convention were greatly alarmed by the persistent discrediting of all radical groups and persons which had gone hand in hand with machine methods for the selection of delegates. The convention seemed to them inoculated in advance against all possible liberalizing influences. The dominating presence of the clergy—there were more than three hundred in a convention of not over a thousand—"all firm allies of M. Dmowski," [15] gave an unfortunate "alien tang" to the discussions. "A significant feature of the convention, which appears to have been dominated by the conservative and clerical elements," said an editorial in the *Nation*, "was the marked opposition to Americanization, at least for the period of the war, as tending to foster indifference to the Polish cause." [16]

As soon as the convention was called to order a self-styled Executive Committee of the National Polish Department appointed a Committee on the Convention consisting of its own personnel or others identified with the same interests. This committee assumed authority to determine the constitution of the convention and the selection of delegates. It also arrogated to itself the right of deciding whether any given organization had complied with certain vaguely worded rules and therefore was entitled to send delegates. These facts alone excluded any "inconvenient" elements.

The delegates assembled, there was little for them to do. The phrase recurring most often was simply "no discussion," and the delegates listened to routine reports and the emotional oratory of

14. Anon., "The Spirit of Poles in America," *Survey, 40* (1918), 721.
15. Irwin Edman, "The Fourth Part of Poland," *Nation, 107* (1918), 342.
16. *Nation, 107* (1918), 281.

Paderewski and Dmowski. The actual business was conducted by seven sectional meetings. The managing committees had prepared, several weeks in advance, the topics for consideration. At the last meeting no discussion was allowed, except upon written request of one-third of the delegates. Paderewski and Dmowski did not wish to take any chances with a packed convention.

By a shrewd political maneuver at the convention all Polish funds were centralized under the pro-Paderewski group, and lest the Poles disown their leaders, the credentials of the delegates were made unconditionally valid for four years. Most significant of all, perhaps, was the marked absence of publicity that attended these decisions vitally affecting almost three million inhabitants of America. Only two papers outside of Detroit, the *New York Evening Post* and the *Christian Science Monitor*, carried reports of the convention.[17] Thus the control of Polish affairs was definitely centered at Paris, and the power of the conservative clique became securely fastened. The Detroit convention, John Dewey reflected, was a story of how "ignorance and emotional knowledge of the past glories of historic Poland combined to make the American Poles readier material for subjection to alien use." [18] It is difficult to imagine a more direct attempt to isolate an immigrant people, a more successful method of doing so, or a more flagrant instance of autocratic alien interference with the affairs of a large domestic population.

When some Polish-Americans attacked the shrouded methods of Paderewski and Dmowski, particularly after John Dewey's article "Autocracy under Cover" appeared in the *New Republic*, the *Wolna Polska*, Paderewski's official organ in America, made a significant statement:

> The most humorous of the plans that have entered upon the public forum via this road is the suggestion that Polish affairs be given over to a Committee of American citizens.
>
> Is there any people in the world, who conscious of its independence and its self respect, would agree to such a proposal? And, furthermore, what people in the world, fighting the worst human tyrant, would invite people to power, who not only have shown no political ripeness but who until recently

17. Irwin Edman, "The Fourth Part of Poland," *Nation, 107* (1918), 342.
18. John Dewey, "Autocracy under Cover," *New Republic, 16* (1918), 103–5. See Appendix.

played with the enemy and accepted financial support from
him. . . .[19]

Many influential Poles, including certain delegates to the Detroit convention, deplored Paderewski's influence on the ground
that "it tended to subordinate the interests of Poland to personal
glorification, but have stated that they were powerless to do anything as long as Mr. Paderewski presented himself to them as having the official support of Great Britain, France and the United
States.[20] In his confidential report to Wilson John Dewey wrote:

> Just as Mr. Dmowski's control of the Detroit Convention
> came, on one hand, from his alleged influence in Europe and
> will, on the other hand, be used to strengthen his power in Eu-
> rope by enabling him to claim that the four million Poles in this
> country are unanimously behind him, so Mr. and Mrs. Pade-
> rewski constantly use their hold on Americans to discourage and
> suppress criticism among the Poles and then, on the other
> hand, employ their supposedly universal popularity among
> the Poles to function more prominently among Americans.[21]

Armed with the "overwhelming support" of the American
Poles, the National Committee increased its political pressure.
Soon after the convention the Pilsudski party in America was ac-
cused of disloyalty. The words "socialist" and "pro-German" were
flung at it. As we have already observed, the Pilsudski party, unlike Dmowski's favored a republic with a democratic form of
government and a moderate socialistic policy. The party had the
support of many peasants and skilled workers. Outside of Poland,
however, it had no official status nor any great influence in Europe,
although in France the majority of Poles who belonged to the
Moderate Democrats were more friendly to it than to the National
Democrats and the Paris Committee. As the strength of the American Polish Committee increased, many American Poles had to
cover their opinions for fear of losing their jobs in munition plants

19. Quoted by Dewey in his confidential report to Wilson. See Dewey to Wilson,
Sept. 25, 1918, Wilson MSS. In this confidential report John Dewey outlined in detail the conditions among the Poles in America and also the manner in which the
Detroit convention was conducted. Wilson did read the excerpt from the *Wolna
Polska* but it is doubtful that he read the Dewey report in its entirety. See Dewey
to Wilson, Sept. 25, 1918; Tumulty to Wilson, Oct. 3, 1918; and Wilson to Dewey,
Oct. 4, 1918; Wilson MSS.
20. Dewey to Wilson, Sept. 25, 1918, Wilson MSS.
21. *Ibid.*

and elsewhere. Since the Polish National Committee had the authority in the United States to identify Poles and issue certificates of Polish nationality to all Poles whom it considered loyal and "irreproachable in conduct," it naturally had tremendous power over the Polish aliens in America.[22] Even Wilson's Administration began to help the committee by banning Polish newspapers and Polish societies of opposite persuasion.[23] But not until January 22, 1919, did the United States give *de jure* recognition to the Paderewski government.[24] Great Britain followed suit on February 26, 1919.

22. On Dec. 20, 1917, Secretary Lansing gave the above authorization to the Polish National Committee. See Lansing to Paderewski, Dec. 20, 1917, *FR:* Supplement 2, *1*, 790.

23. Baker, *Woodrow Wilson, 8,* 223. See also *FR: 1918,* Supplement 2, p. 206.

24. *FR: 1919, 2,* 741.

8. Wilson and Dmowski

WHEN DMOWSKI ARRIVED in America, the first thing he asked Paderewski was "How are affairs going?" "Badly," replied Paderewski, "both with public opinion and with the Government." This pessimistic impression, as we have learned from the previous chapter, was not exaggerated. Dmowski, however, was not so concerned as Paderewski. "When I have to deal with influential enemies," the self-assured president of the Paris Polish National Committee remarked, "I immediately attempt to seek other sources of influence to nullify their adverse affect." "I went to Detroit," Dmowski wrote in his memoirs, ". . . and that was a good beginning." [1] After the Detroit convention the picture changed. As the official spokesman of American and European Poles and armed with the ostensible support of "four million" American Poles, Dmowski was ready to see Wilson.

Paderewski and Dmowski were not so much concerned over Wilson's reluctance to recognize Polish independence as over his attitude toward the frontiers of the new Poland. By September 1918, the two representatives of the Polish National Committee were confident that Poland would be re-established. What worried them was the future boundaries of Poland, and especially what Wilson meant by "a free and secure access to the sea." This question decided Dmowski to call upon the president.

Dmowski's first audience took place in the White House on Friday, September 13, 1918.[2] He was accompanied by Paderewski. The conversation entered on the question of "free access to the sea," which Wilson had promised in his address on the Fourteen Points on January 8, 1918. By "free access to the sea," Dmowski records in his memoirs, Wilson did not necessarily mean a territorial corridor to the Baltic. The revelation is particularly interesting when one recalls that the dispute over the Polish Corridor furnished Hitler with a pretext for his attack on Poland in 1939.

1. Dmowski, *Polityka Polska,* p. 388.
2. Entry of Sept. 13, 1918 in Wilson's Appointment Book which reads: "Mr. Paderewski to present Mr. Roman Demowski [*sic*] 4:30–5:00," Wilson MSS. "After our departure from Detroit," wrote Dmowski, "Paderewski obtained an interview with the President for both of us, and we set out for Washington." Roman Dmowski, *Polityka Polska,* p. 389.

According to Dmowski the conversation with Wilson lasted nearly an hour and a half.[3] "I found him," Dmowski wrote,

> to be a man of great culture, pleasant manners, very willing to debate, listening with attention to the arguments of his inter-locutor, seeking to form his own opinion on the subject of dis-cussion. At the same time, however, I discovered that he did not know much about Polish affairs, that he did not understand European politics, that he simplified too much their most com-plex aspects, that he had a great faith in the possibility of set-tling international problems on the basis of justice enforced upon all.[4]

Dmowski's skepticism over the effectiveness of a law binding all nations must not be taken as proof of any great foresight, since his memoirs were written in 1925. It proves only that Dmowski, who prided himself on his realism, did not share Wilson's desire to build a brave new world but wanted only to assure a new Poland a safe place in the old one. Wilson's bold dreams merely exasperated him. The president of the Polish National Committee, before recording his conversation with Wilson, boasted that he was well prepared for the meeting with the president of the United States. "I was warned in Europe," he wrote, "by a person, who knew the Presi-dent personally, not to speak of politics in the conventional terms of frontier adjustments, strategy and prestige, and especially not to use the term, 'balance of power' for he cannot stand it."

"Knowing how Wilson understood 'free access to the sea,'" Dmowski confessed, "I emphasized this subject during our conver-sation and explained to him our aspirations and our rights to a sea coast." He showed the president that the population of Pomorze, like that of Poznania and Upper Silesia, was in the great majority Polish; and "that only a territorial access could be a free and secure access to the sea. . . ."

"But," observed Wilson, "would it not be sufficient for you if the Lower Vistula and the free port of Danzig were neutralized?"

"Mr. President," Dmowski replied, "that is as though you had said to us: You will have full liberty to breathe, but the Germans will have you by the throat. . . ." Then Dmowski proceeded to point out the lack of realism in such a proposed settlement from

---

3. According to Wilson's Appointment Book the visit lasted only a half hour. Wilson MSS.

4. Dmowski, *Polityka Polska*, pp. 389–90.

the political as well as from the economic point of view, and "presently began to speak of strategic considerations."

"My dear Mr. Dmowski," Wilson interrupted, "who, after this war will talk any more of strategic considerations? After all we shall have the League of Nations. . . ."

"I believe in the League of Nations," replied Dmowski, "as I believe in the justice of the United States. To guarantee it you need not only laws and tribunals, but also police and prisons. . . ."

"But we shall have an international police force," Wilson put in.

"Who is going to create it? Will you maintain the American Army in Europe? Such a police force could only be formed by local armies of their [i.e., German] neighbors. France alone will be too weak for it on account of the disproportion between her population and that of Germany. . . . You know well that if there is an unsafe quarter in town, extra police are sent there. Well, Central and Eastern Europe is an unsafe quarter. Poland, in order to safeguard peace and her security, will be called upon to make a great effort. We cannot forget strategic considerations. If the League of Nations wishes to gain in respect and importance we must be strong and fit to defend ourselves."

"The conversation," Dmowski recalled, "was carried on in a very affable tone. It ended with Wilson's suggesting that I furnish him with maps of the Polish state as we would like to see it, accompanied by notes explaining about every province, why we needed it, what importance it would have for the future state, and what rights we had to it."

If we are to believe Dmowski, the only contribution Paderewski made during the interview was his allusion to the fact that Poland had been dealt with in the thirteenth point and therefore he hoped "that this would not bring bad luck to the future state." The president, according to Dmowski, assured the pianist he had always considered thirteen his lucky number.[5]

Immediately upon his arrival in the United States Dmowski had learned from two Polish members of the Inquiry, Dr. Henryk Arctowski and Professor S. J. Zowski,[6] that the Polish section of

5. *Ibid.,* pp. 389–92.

6. "Shortly after my conversation with the President," wrote Dmowski, "I learned a new fact which had been kept secret. There already existed in the United States a group of experts under the direction of Colonel House whose task was to

the Inquiry had not received instructions to assemble data about the territory later known as the Polish Corridor. From this he concluded that the Americans did not intend it for Poland. The president clarified his position about "free and secure access to the sea" in an address to the Senate on January 22, 1917:

> So far as practicable, moreover, every great people now struggling toward a full development of its resources and of its powers should be assured a direct outlet to the highway of the sea. Where this cannot be done by cession of territory, it can no doubt be done by the neutralization of direct rights of way under the general guarantee which will assure the peace itself. With a right comity of arrangement no nation need be shut away from free access to the open paths of the world's commerce.[7]

Shortly after the interview with the president, Dmowski, aware that the question of territorial access to the sea was "not yet sufficiently understood by the best-informed Americans," asked the Polish National Council of Chicago to organize a campaign that ought to "culminate in a resolution demanding the creation of a Polish state which should embrace not only Poznania and Silesia, but also Pomorze and Danzig." He also issued orders to influence the American press.[8] On September 14, after seeing Robert Lansing, he made a special visit to Boston where he lunched with Colonel House and Professor Roscoe W. Thayer of Harvard. "House was silent throughout," Dmowski recalled, "he only listened to my conversation with the historian Thayer." [9] In his diary Colonel House recorded:

> Dmowski, President of the National Polish Council which sits in Paris, lunched with us. We had a long and satisfactory talk —something we were unable to do when he called on me in Paris. I had so much to do there that I could ask him [only] to give me a memorandum. . . .

prepare material for the American delegates to the Peace Conference. In this, so-called House Commission, there was a Polish section under the chairmanship of Professor Lord, author of the book on the Polish partition. In this section there were also two Poles, Professors Zwierzchowski and Arctowski." *Ibid.*, p. 392.

7. Arthur B. Tourtellot, *Woodrow Wilson Selections for Today* (New York, Duell, Sloan and Pearce, 1945), p. 133.

8. Dmowski, *Polityka Polska*, pp. 394–5.

9. *Ibid.*, p. 392.

We talked of Poland and her future. We discussed the possible boundaries for the new Poland and its form of government. He believes if Germany and Russia are monarchies, a Polish republic would not live between them. Poland, he believes, in that case, would have to become a monarchy, although a liberal one. He did not think a Pole could be selected for King because of factional differences. A King he thought would have to be sought in another country.[10]

Dmowski submitted to the president on October 8, 1918, his memorandum on the frontiers of the Polish state and a map showing the frontiers desired by the National Committee. In this memorandum he demanded the whole corridor, Danzig and Upper Silesia.[11] The president did not take any action. Neither he nor Colonel House had a definite plan for the future Polish frontiers. Not until later at Paris did Wilson make up his mind on the question of the corridor and Danzig.

The Armistice surprised and displeased Dmowski. He thought it premature, wishing that the Allies had marched into Berlin and into Central Europe. He could not comprehend the boundless joy of the New Yorkers shown during the False Armistice (November 7). He hastened to Washington. When he was shown the Armistice terms with Germany he was further enraged. There were two articles that concerned Poland.[12] Article 16 provided for free communication between the Allied countries and Poland through the Baltic and Danzig. "That was the only logical thing in the whole illogical situation in which the Armistice left Poland," Dmowski commented, and added cynically, "And that is probably why it was not put in effect." Article 12 provided for immediate evacuation by the Germans of territories seized in the East during the war. He was less satisfied with this provision: "In my mind I saw the position of Poland. There is no Polish Army at home, the Allies have not come with their armies, the German Army is retreating to Germany and in its place the Bolshevik flood is pouring in from the East." [13]

On Armistice Day Dmowski was invited to listen to President Wilson's special address to the Senate:

10. House diary, Sept. 14, 1918.
11. Dmowski to Wilson, Oct. 8, 1918, Wilson MSS.
12. *FR: 1918,* Supplement 1, *1,* 463–8.
13. Dmowski, *Polityka Polska,* p. 400–2.

While I sat there in the midst of the American senators and listened to the President's speech, thoughts were passing through my mind. Among these respected men of the Great Republic exceptions were those who understood what was going on in Europe. I knew among them only one who did, an old Senator of the Republican Party, Lodge. His party had a few men looking realistically at the international situation, such as Elihu Root or the former President Roosevelt . . . but it had no influence then on the foreign policy of the United States. It was Wilson who decided, and he wanted to establish general peace and justice among nations under the auspices of the League of Nations. Meanwhile, he brought the war to a premature end resulting in chaos out of which Europe would not get out soon.[14]

Such was Dmowski's opinion of Poland's "miracle man."

A half hour after the Senate had adjourned President Wilson received Dmowski at the White House for a farewell audience.[15] Following a brief discussion of the Armistice Convention Dmowski turned the conversation to Polish affairs and to the question of the German-Polish boundary, "hoping," he wrote, "to get from him an express assurance." Wilson answered reluctantly, expressing many reservations. "His mind seemed rather set against our claims. . . . I saw that somebody must have worked against our interests. . . . I did not want to part with him leaving our affairs in such a state. I used therefore the last argument."

"Mr. President," Dmowski quotes himself as saying, "do you know how the American Poles look at this question? The men, who are their leaders, come mostly from Polish lands seized by the Prussians. Therefore if we do not get a proper boundary against Germany, if we do not get not only Posen but also Silesia and our Baltic land with Danzig, none of them will understand why. And those are people who today have deep faith in you."

"Wilson gave me a deep look and said in a firm voice: 'I have hopes that they will not be disappointed.' "[16] "Despite the threat to turn the Polish vote against him," Dyboski wrote, "Wilson did not commit himself."[17]

14. *Ibid.,* pp. 400–1.
15. Wilson's "Appointment Book," Nov. 11, 1918, Wilson MSS.
16. Dmowski, *Polityka Polska,* pp. 401–2.
17. Dyboski, "The Polish Question during the World War," in W. F. Reddaway, *Cambridge History of Poland,* p. 489. Dmowski·believed that Wilson owed his elec-

After his fruitless visit with Wilson Dmowski saw House in Paris. Frazier, a member of the American Embassy staff, informed Pronczak of the Paris Polish National Committee that "Colonel House will be exceedingly glad to see Mr. Dmowski and looks forward to seeing the maps of the proposed frontiers of Poland. The Colonel also directs me to say that he will not fail to call upon you for any information which he may be in need of regarding the Polish situation." [18] A few weeks later, December 4, Dmowski and House discussed Polish affairs and the formation of the new Polish state.[19]

Dmowski's last meeting with Wilson occurred at a farewell dinner in Paris before the president left the conference for America. According to Dmowski the president said: "Do you remember when I asked you in Washington for the maps of the future Poland? Well, you did not get everything, but you must admit that what you did get is not so far from what you had asked. I did all I could." "I am sure," Dmowski concluded, "he wanted to do more." [20]

tion to the Polish vote. "The count of votes after the second election of Wilson revealed that he would not have been elected if several central states had fallen away from him, in which Polish votes were of great importance." Dmowski, *Polityka Polska*, p. 293.

18. Frazier to Pronozak (Pronczak), Nov. 22, 1918. House MSS.
19. House diary, Dec. 4, 1918.
20. Dmowski, *Polityka Polska*, p. 402.

9. Restoration

THE COLLAPSE of the three partitioning powers set the stage for the national restoration of Poland, but not for immediate unity and independence. The German request of October 4 for a general armistice on Wilson's terms found the Poles in Poland unprepared for the task of organizing a united government. Chaos and confusion followed in the wake of the German and Austrian retreat. In the north the Bolsheviks held Vilna. The Ukrainians held Eastern Galicia, from Lwow to the Russian frontier. The Germans continued to rule Poznania. In Lublin the Socialist leader Ignace Daszynski formed a Socialist government and declared a republic. In Western Galicia a Polish Committee assumed authority over the Austrian area.

The situation in Poland continued to be precarious until the arrival of Joseph Pilsudski in Warsaw on November 10, 1918. His release from the Magdeburg fortress marked the beginning of centralization of authority on Polish soil. His popularity among the Polish masses and soldiery was great. Poland indeed was fortunate to have so charismatic a personality in command on the eve of its rebirth. Within a few days after his arrival the Lublin government acknowledged Pilsudski's authority. The Polish general became chief of state, and Daszynski his premier. On November 16 Pilsudski brushed aside all opposition and notified the powers that a free Polish state had come into existence.

Pilsudski's rapid action in establishing himself as independent ruler did not conform to the realities existing inside as well as outside Poland. Many Polish political groups refused to acknowledge his leadership. Substantial segments of Polish territory were held by foreign troops and native insurrectionists. Moreover, the whole matter of Polish frontiers remained in doubt.

Of greatest concern to the emerging Polish state was the Polish National Committee's hostile and uncompromising attitude toward Pilsudski. In Allied capitals it was Dmowski who represented Poland. Why the Quai d'Orsay supported Dmowski, the political opportunist and reactionary, it is not difficult to understand. The subtle, polished, and imperialistic Dmowski appeared to the French as a man to be encouraged. In his exaggerated territorial demands the French Foreign Office saw an opportunity to reduce future threats from Germany by building a strong Poland on her eastern border. The future Poland was to take the place of the old tsarist Russia, now lost to France. But it would be a mistake to say that France wholeheartedly supported Polish territorial claims in the east. As long as there was still hope that Russia might be won back as an ally France did not wish to antagonize her irrevocably. Nor did the French Government support the Poles in their disputes with the Czechs. Within these restrictions the Quai d'Orsay was for a Poland "grande et forte, très forte," as Pichon declared.[1] The French attitude can be gauged from the following editorial in the *Temps:* "If the wish of the Poles is satisfied, the French public will be particularly satisfied. France cannot forget that the understanding between Alexander I and William I on the Polish rising in 1863 had prepared the way for Sadowa, Sedan and the annexation of Alsace-Lorraine by the German Empire. Justice will rule on the Rhine only if it rules on the Vistula." [2]

The French Government did not want a Poland governed by Socialist Pilsudski. Socialism meant bolshevism, and for this reason Dmowski, because of his association with the late tsar, was supported by the French Foreign Office as against Pilsudski, who was regarded as a Socialist agitator. Immediately after Pilsudski had succeeded in establishing a government on Polish soil, Pichon was ready to proclaim the Polish National Committee in Paris as the de facto government of Poland [3] British opposition stopped him.

The British Foreign Office considered Pichon's design premature and dangerous. Balfour feared lest recognition of the Polish National Committee as the legitimate government of Poland not only alienate Polish public opinion in Poland but also orient the Warsaw government toward Germany.[4]

Although Britain sincerely favored the restoration of an independent Poland, she did not favor the idea of a strong and big Polish state. The British disliked Dmowski's group, which they considered to be working in the interest of reactionary forces in Poland rather than for the masses of the Polish people. "In fact," Lord

1. Robert H. Lord, "Poland," in Edward M. House and Charles Seymour, eds., *What Really Happened at Paris* (New York, 1921), pp. 69–71.

2. Quoted by J. H. Harley, "Poland's Hour of Destiny," *Polish Review, 2* (London, 1918).

3. Joseph Blociszewski, *La Restauration de la Pologne et la diplomatie européene* (Paris, 1927), p. 140.

4. *Ibid.*, pp. 140 and 143.

Howard of Penrith wrote, "the prevailing opinion at the time seemed to be that to do anything the Polish Committee asked for would be to fasten upon Poland a *regime* of wicked landlords who spent most of their time in riotous living, and establish there a chauvinist Government whose object was to acquire territories inhabited by non-Polish populations." [5]

British refusal temporarily shattered the hopes of the leaders of the Polish National Committee, who were bent on becoming the undisputed masters of Poland. When on December 4 Dmowski discussed this problem with House, he was urged to moderate his views and settle on a coalition government.[6] A few days later he made it known that he wished to reach an agreement with Pilsudski in regard to the formation of a unified and representative government. France and Great Britain welcomed the announcement and promised to help.

Dmowski's change of heart was only a ruse to negate British opposition to him, for at no time did he wish to share his power with General Pilsudski. The head of the Polish National Committee remained convinced that during the ensuing negotiations Pilsudski would be relegated to a minor position. In these calculations and hopes the United States played an important role. A Paderewski government was established. Wilson had made it possible.

The man chosen by Dmowski to go to Poland was Paderewski. In December 1918 the pianist arrived in Paris, where he conferred with the French Government, but mainly with Dmowski.[7] Together they drafted a memorandum formulating Poland's proposed attitudes during the forthcoming Peace Conference. From Paris Paderewski went to London. There he saw Lord Balfour who wished him success in his mission "to unite Polish hearts" so that Poland might be "properly represented at the Peace Conference."

Recognizing the importance of British support, Paderewski asked that a British warship be assigned to take him to Danzig. Again he went to Paris to see Dmowski, who was delighted with what he had accomplished; then he returned to London to board the warship.

Backed by the prestige of the British cruiser *Condor*, a British chargé d'affaires, Colonel H. H. Wade, who accompanied him, and

5. Sir Esme W. Howard, *Theatre of Life* (London, Holder and Stoughton, 1936), pp. 649–52.
6. Seymour, *Intimate Papers, 4,* 239.
7. Landau, *Paderewski,* p. 118.

the ostensible claim that he represented, and was entrusted with power of attorney from, the "four million Poles" in America, Paderewski was certain that he would be able to seize control of the new state of Poland.[8]

He landed at Danzig on Christmas Day, 1918, and immediately took advantage of the favorable position which the British cruiser and Colonel Wade afforded him. Instead of going directly to Warsaw he decided to stop first at Posen, thus signifying to the Germans that the territory of Poznania, legally Prussian, was to be incorporated into the new Poland. As soon as German officials at Danzig learned of the change of plans they tried to induce the two men to proceed to Warsaw via Thorn. Paderewski and Wade insisted on going to Posen.

A representative of the German General Staff in civilian clothes boarded their train on the way to Posen. He repeated to Colonel Wade that his safe conduct called for transit through Germany to Warsaw via Thorn, and asked them not to go to Posen. Colonel Wade refused.

Paderewski's arrival in Poznania was well timed. On the same day a hastily raised Polish force started an uprising under General Dowbor-Nusnicki and for a time gained control over some parts of the territory later to be claimed by Poland. Paderewski and his British escort were at first well received by the people of Posen, but on the following day German soldiers and anti-Paderewski Poles stormed the offices of the Polish National Council, tore down Polish and Allied flags, and fired into Paderewski's room.[9] Desultory fighting continued until at the Conference of Trèves in February 1919 the Allies laid down a temporary line of demarcation.

On New Year's Day Paderewski arrived in Warsaw, where great crowds waited for him. "It would have been wonderful," Landau wrote, "if another man [Pilsudski] had not been received with

8. "In sending to Poland on a British cruiser," wrote Barnes, "a member of the discredited and denounced Paris committee—which the world now knows as monarchical, representative of conservative economic interests, . . .—and to support that member in attempts to seize an orderly and self-determined government, the Allied governments have the stage fully set for outbreak of Bolshevism of the most virulent type." Albert C. Barnes, "The Paderewski Adventure," *New Republic, 17* (1919), 367–9.

9. See Osborne's memorandum, Jan. 1, 1919, *FR: Paris Peace Conference, 1919, 2,* 423–4.

In his dispatch to the British Foreign Office Colonel Wade, after observing conditions in Poznania and learning of Paderewski's territorial ambitions, indicated that he was not in complete accord with Paderewski's ideas as to the territorial extent of Poland; he regarded them as exaggerated. *Ibid.*

similar enthusiasm when he entered Warsaw a few weeks before." [10]

Paderewski's task in Poland, as Landau stated, was to bridge the gulf between Dmowski and Pilsudski, "between Poland in the East and Poland in the West." In this endeavor he did not succeed. The first meeting between Pilsudski and Paderewski took place at Pilsudski's residence on January 4. The aristocratic Paderewski was shocked to find no butlers, footmen, or other servants such as one might expect in the palace of the chief of state. The soldiers on guard looked with curious eyes at Paderewski as he alighted from his motor car, wearing a small brown felt hat and costly fur coat, with long sable collar and sable cuffs, that reached almost to the ground.[11] Pilsudski's appearance did not please Paderewski. His greying mustache was neglected and too long; his gray tunic was actually shabby. "When both men rose after a long conversation," Landau wrote, "Paderewski knew that no understanding was possible, and not merely because of political opinion. It was as though two planets had tried to revolve on the same orbit." [12]

The West soon learned of Paderewski's unsuccessful attempt to persuade Pilsudski either to retire or to make him premier of Poland. Paderewski described his meeting with Pilsudski to Lieut. R. C. Foster of the Coolidge Commission.[13] He stated that the Pilsudski government was unpopular, inefficient and incompetent, and for proof pointed to what he called Pilsudski's unwillingness to compromise! [14] He also reported that Pilsudski had suggested he form a cabinet but that he had refused to do so. The statement is of dubious truth. In his *Poprawki Historyczne (Historical Corrections)* Pilsudski makes it quite plain that he did not at their first meeting offer Paderewski the premiership. On the contrary he did not even wish to include Paderewski in his government. The general wrote:

A certain Doctor Paderewski, known representative of the National Democratic party in Warsaw, came to see me. Since I

10. Landau, *Paderewski,* p. 128.
11. *Ibid.,* p. 136.
12. *Ibid.,* p. 137.
13. The Coolidge Commission took its name from its chief, Professor Archibald C. Coolidge. It was organized by the Allied Powers at the Peace Conference for the purpose of obtaining information and data about conditions in Central Europe.
14. On Jan. 29, 1919, Dmowski completely contradicted this statement of Paderewski. Before the Council of Ten Dmowski said: "Pilsudski had become very popular as he had fought against Russia in the beginning of the war and afterwards had been imprisoned by the Germans." *See FR: Paris Peace Conference, 1919, 3,* 775.

was in bed with a slight fever I received him in my bedroom. This individual began to tell me of the impossibility of the National Democratic party's working with Mr. Daszynski. . . . While arguing against Daszynski he made loathsome and disparaging remarks against him. Finally I interrupted this flow of venom, reproved him for his previous actions, and ended all talk with him.[15]

What were the reasons for Paderewski's professed refusal to form a government under Pilsudski? In his conference with Foster he explained that Pilsudski had been made head of the government by the Regency, and since the Germans had put the Regency in power Pilsudski represented a German influence. Therefore, if Paderewski undertook to form a cabinet under Pilsudski, "he would not be working thro(ugh) [the] wish of the people but under the auspices of the old German influence."

This statement was absurd. It was precisely because of Pilsudski's refusal to take an oath of allegiance to the German and Austrian emperors that he was jailed at Magdeburg. What is more important, on October 8, 1918, the Regency Council at Warsaw dissolved the Council of State which had been elected under German auspices, and on the 22d of that month summoned a new cabinet under Swierzynski, largely National Democratic and hence anti-German in color! [16]

At the end of his conference with Pilsudski Paderewski, aware of the West's fear of bolshevism, charged that the Bolsheviks were the power behind "Pilsudski's throne." The charge was false, but it strengthened his plea for Polish troops to be sent from abroad.[17]

On January 16 Pilsudski was forced to change his mind, and Paderewski became premier of Poland. The men who were responsible for this startling reversal were Woodrow Wilson and Herbert Hoover.

15. Jozef Pilsudski, *Poprawki,* pp. 84–5.
16. H. H. Fisher and Sidney Brooks, *America and the New Poland,* p. 115.
17. Lieut. R. C. Foster to Prof. A. C. Coolidge, Warsaw, Jan. 9, 1919, *FR: Paris Peace Conference, 17,* 365–7.
Paderewski's attempt to influence the representative of the American commission which was sent to investigate conditions in Central Europe was not quite successful. After Paderewski's conference with Pilsudski Lieutenant Foster decided to see the general. He sent the following report to Professor Coolidge after the meeting: "My whole impression of Pilsudski was that he was working for Poland and he spoke with a certain force and conviction that I had not expected to find as a result of the impressions given me by other people. . . ." See Foster to Coolidge, Jan. 9, 1919, *ibid.,* p. 369.

Two important events occurred in Warsaw on the day that Paderewski and Pilsudski met for the first time. The first was an abortive coup d'état against Pilsudski; the second was the arrival of the American Food Mission. On the evening of January 4, after Pilsudski had refused to hand over the government to Paderewski, a small detachment of troops led by Prince Sapieha tried to overthrow the Socialist government.[18] Three members of the cabinet were arrested by a group of the Polish militia that had been brought into the scheme. They also arrested the chief of staff of the army, General Szeptycki, but when he persuaded his jailers that this act would demoralize the army, they let him go. The general went at once to Pilsudski, who immediately released the ministers, arrested Prince Sapieha, and sent Szeptycki to Cracow to bring Paderewski to Warsaw.

Polish historians have attributed Paderewski's assumption of the premiership to the Sapieha conspiracy. Even H. H. Fisher and Sidney Brooks have implied that it was a decisive factor.[19] This abortive *putsch*, however, failed to bring about a change in the Polish Government. A closer examination of the facts shows that the coup d'état was directed not so much against Pilsudski, who was generally respected as a patriot of great political ability, as against his Socialist cabinet. That Pilsudski was not distressed by · the attempt to overthrow his government is shown by the fact that when Paderewski arrived in Warsaw on January 5 he found, to his dismay, the Socialist ministers still in power. Moreover, in the ensuing conference with Paderewski General Pilsudski held out for an entire Socialist cabinet. As a matter of fact, Professor Coolidge wrote to the Commission to Negotiate Peace, "the *coup d'état* has strengthened the present socialistic government on account of its failure." [20]

The decisive factor which brought pressure on Pilsudski to agree to bring in Paderewski was not the Sapieha conspiracy but the Hoover Food Mission. This fact has been either completely overlooked or greatly minimized. On January 4, the day of the

18. Paderewski knew of this coup d'état but he did not participate in it. After his fruitless conversation with Pilsudski he left for Cracow in the new Cadillac Herbert Hoover had given him. This new American-made car impressed many Poles who flocked to see it. It also indicated to them, of course, that America was behind Paderewski. See Aniela Strakacz, *Paderewski As I Knew Him*, p. 34.

19. Fisher and Brooks, *America and the New Poland*, p. 122.

20. Prof. A. C. Coolidge to the Commission to Negotiate Peace, Vienna, Jan. 11, 1919, *FR: Paris Peace Conference, 2*, 229–33. See also Lieut. R. C. Foster to Professor Coolidge, Warsaw, Jan. 9, 1919, *ibid.*, pp. 365–7.

abortive coup d'état, Dr. Vernon Kellogg and Col. William R. Grove, who headed the Polish section of the Hoover Food Mission, arrived in Warsaw, accompanied by Jan Horodyski, the British Pole who had gone with Wiseman to the United States. "Without waiting for the outcome of these [Pilsudski-Paderewski] conversations," Fisher asserted, "and without attempting to bring to bear any of the tremendous pressure which their position placed in their hands, they began discussions of the food situation with the Chief of State, the Prime Minister, the Ministers of Approvisation, Agriculture, Railways and Finance, the President of the City of Warsaw and various delegations of citizens." [21]

Fisher's emphatic statement that the American Food Mission did not exert any pressure on Pilsudski does not agree with the facts. During the two weeks following January 4 the presence of the mission attracted the attention of the Polish public. Some of its members were in the uniform of officers of the American Army. The mission held daily conferences with ministers and officials who were deeply concerned with the famine which had left millions of Poles destitute and which threatened to destroy Poland's social structure. The Polish newspapers reported these conferences in detail. Dr. Kellogg himself, in an article for the *World's Work*, reveals that his mission spoke "authoritatively" with Pilsudski. Kellogg wrote:

> One point in all the negotiations was emphasized. It was a suggestive point. It was plainly indicated that no food could come from America or the Allies on a wholesale scale if there was any serious danger that it could not be properly controlled. . . . This all meant that food relief—imperatively needed to keep Poland alive and free from that push of misery that meant revolution and Bolshevism—could only be hoped for in the presence of a government so truly representative and so universally accepted by the people that it could be relied on by America and the Allies to keep order and maintain a safe control of the imported foodstuffs. . . . [22]

All this, Kellogg said, was free of politics. But after denying any political ties, Dr. Kellogg betrayed himself in his incongruous conclusion: "Food and politics had an inevitable and inseparable con-

21. Fisher and Brooks, *America and the New Poland*, p. 126.
22. Vernon Kellogg, "Paderewski, Pilsudski, and Poland," *World's Work, 38* (1919), 109–12.

nection ever since the beginning of the war; and they have it still. And all during the week of the *coup d'état* and food negotiations Paderewski was talking with Pilsudski." [23]

What did Paderewski say to Pilsudski? While no records of these conversations survive there is no doubt that he pointed out how the Allies could do nothing for Poland in the way of relief, military supplies, or financial support unless Pilsudski's government included the Conservatives and was headed by Paderewski. The pianist could certainly speak with authority. For now he had in his possession a letter from Hoover endorsed by President Wilson which categorically stated that aid would be extended to Poland as long as he was in charge.[24] Moreover President Wilson saw to it that throughout these conferences not even a "superficial idea" was to be given that "M. Paderewski was not being supported." [25]

No wonder Pilsudski, needing American relief for the starving people of Poland and wishing to utilize the friendship of Paderewski with the Allied leaders for the benefit of Poland, decided to bring him into the government.[26] Thus Paderewski became prime

23. *Ibid.*, p. 112. Herbert Hoover in his *Memoirs* contradicts Dr. Kellogg's assertion: "Dr. Kellogg asked that he be authorized to inform Pilsudski that unless this was done [place Paderewski at the head of the government] American cooperation and aid were futile. I did so and got the hint reinforced from President Wilson. As a result Pilsudski was elevated to the position of 'Chief of State,' and Paderewski became Prime Minister on January 16th." *The Memoirs of Herbert Hoover* (New York, Macmillan, 1951), p. 357.

24. The stenographic report read: "President Wilson said that M. Paderewski had a letter in his possession from Mr. Hoover, informing him that aid would only be extended to Poland so long as he was in charge." See Notes of a Meeting Held at President Wilson's House in Paris, May 17, 1919, *FR: Paris Peace Conference, 1919, 5,* 676. This letter was later reinforced by a personal letter from President Wilson to Paderewski which was written for the president's signature by Colonel House. In the House diary for May 5, 1919, we find the following statement: "The President said he had signed and sent the letter I wrote for him to send Paderewski. I am glad of this because there is a fight made upon Paderewski in Poland and this letter may save the situation." See also House to Wilson, April 23, 1919, House MSS.

25. "President Wilson said it was important not to give even a superficial idea that M. Paderewski was not being supported. He had played the game straight throughout. The message ought to be sent, not to M. Paderewski, but to General Pilsudski, the Head of the Polish State." *Ibid.*, p. 677.

26. Immediately after the news of Paderewski's appointment reached Paris, President Wilson, through Secretary Lansing, sent his best wishes and gave Paderewski his assurance that it would be "a source of gratification to enter into official relations with you at the earliest opportunity; and to render to your country such aid as it is possible at this time. . . ." Lansing to Paderewski, Jan. 22, 1919, Fisher and Brooks, *America and the New Poland,* p. 357. It is worth noting that on Jan. 22 the Allies recognized the Paderewski government.

minister, foreign secretary, and Poland's delegate—together with Dmowski whom Pilsudski despised—to the Peace Conference.[27] The parties of the Polish *Sejm*, however, continued to oppose him. Paderewski's power depended on the presence of the American Relief Mission.[28] Significantly enough, when the Hoover Mission left Poland late in 1919, Paderewski lost his premiership (December 7, 1919) and voluntarily exiled himself from the country.

27. Dluski, Pilsudski's appointee, was only an alternate.
28. See Landau, *Paderewski*, p. 141. See also Baker, *Woodrow Wilson, 8,* 163.

10. Poland Reborn Expands

To THE DISTRACTED Polish exiles, who since 1831 had been dispersed all over Europe, Poland stood for an ideal as well as for a territory. The Poland of the émigré's dreams was not a Polish national state but the old Poland as it existed before the first partition of 1772. Even during the early years of the first World War, before there was any likelihood of a free, united, and independent Poland, the dream of a large Polish empire still obsessed the minds of the Polish nobility and some members of the intelligentsia.

Those Polish leaders who supported Germany and Austria and believed implicitly in their promises of a future autonomous Poland dreamt of a vast empire stretching to the gates of Smolensk and Kiev and including the whole of Lithuania, nearly all of White Russia, with parts of Latvia and the western Ukraine. This "Greater Polish State" is usually referred to as Jagiellonian Poland because it was under the Jagiellonian dynasty that Poland attained its farthest expansion eastward. The Jagiellonians, who came from Lithuania, reigned in Poland for almost two centuries (1386–1572). Their policy appealed so much to many Polish nobles that they adopted it and handed it down from generation to generation as a national testament. To Pilsudski, member of the Lithuanian nobility and early supporter of Germany and Austria against Russia, fell the task of realizing the vision of his predecessors.

It would be logical to expect that the Polish nobles, who owned vast plains in old Poland, would become the main protagonists of the Jagiellonian idea. But what of the liberal and socialistic elements of the Polish emigration? What of the Socialist Pilsudski? Did they too champion a Poland within the frontiers of 1772? They supported it, but for quite other reasons. The Polish liberals and their European sympathizers declared themselves for a Poland of maximum size, because this would imply a restriction of the territory held by tsarist Russia, fountainhead of European reaction. As a Socialist agitator Pilsudski had contemplated the probability of Estonia, Livonia, Lithuania, Ukraine, and White Russia becoming independent states, and looked forward to voluntary federation later. But when he became head of the Polish state, he immediately embarked on forceful incorporation of these territories.

111

In this he was supported by the Polish nobility and large landowners who, seeing their property in those territories which the Jagiellonian program embraced submerged by the Bolshevik deluge, hoped by realization of that program to regain them.

The Jagiellonian program was not the sum total of Polish national aspirations. Alongside it there appeared, sometimes as an alternative, often as a combination, the Piast idea of diverting Polish expansionist tendencies toward the West, while retaining the Jagiellonian belief in the excellence of the old Poland. Piast is the name of the legendary Slav peasant who is considered the founder of the first Polish ruling house. It was not to this legend that Polish nationalists looked back when evoking the Piast idea, but rather to Poland's first king, Mieszko I, Piast's great-grandson. Mieszko I (963–992) founded a Polish state that included territory beyond the Oder in the west, and the Baltic coast between the Oder and the mouth of the Vistula in the north. In the east it did not pass the Bug, and in the south ended at the Carpathian Mountains.

The second national idea was taken up primarily by those Poles who supported tsarist Russia. The heir and advocate of the Piast conception was Roman Dmowski.[1] The main territorial attraction for the leader of the National Democratic party lay in Silesia, East Prussia, and the wide outlet to the sea. Immediately after the outbreak of the World War Dmowski turned the Poles' attention to the danger of thinking in terms of large areas to be gained on the eastern borders and directed them westward—to German territories, "the cradle of the Polish race." The pro-tsarist Dmowski, convinced of the sincerity of the Russian promises concerning the future state of Poland, was willing to sacrifice historic claims to eastern Poland in return for western lands long occupied and settled by Germans. The adherents of the Piast idea pointed to the natural role of Poland in forming a bridge between the Black Sea and the Baltic, and the "predominant character" which the rivers flowing into the Baltic, the Oder, Vistula, and Niemen assume in the Polish landscape.[2] During the early years of the first World War imperialist Russia encouraged the Poles to think in Piast terms, while Germany and Austria, in their own interest, pushed Poland along the Jagiellonian path.[3]

1. See Dmowski, *La Question polonaise,* pp. 310–13.
2. See H. Baginski, *Poland and the Baltic: the Problem of Poland's Access to the Sea* (London, 1942), p. 185.
3. Today we are again witnessing very concentrated propaganda of Soviet Russia to interest the Poles in the Piast dreams. Most of the historical literature in

When tsarist Russia was defeated in the war and destroyed at home by the Bolshevik Revolution, the Piast conception ceased to be an alternative idea. For Dmowski it was now possible to evoke and add the Jagiellonian conception to his plan for the future Poland. Once this was done he began to talk freely of a Poland that included Ukrainians, White Russians, Czechs, Germans, Lithuanians, and Latvians. Even before Poland became independent, and while she still needed the help of Wilson who brought the United States into the war to "make the world safe for Democracy," Dmowski made known his desire to resurrect the Poland of prepartition days—"ruled" by foreign kings but controlled by the nobility.[4]

Colonel House knew of Dmowski's aspirations, but failed to make him modify his views. So did Stephen Bonsal, assistant to House, who also realized that Dmowski's Poland was "the old Poland with its manor farms stretching from the Baltic to the Black Sea" and ruled by "gallant knights." [5] President Wilson, however, did not learn of Dmowski's conception of the new Poland, which he helped to resurrect, until the Peace Conference.

The power vacuum created in Central Europe by the Bolshevik Revolution and the defeat of the Central Powers gave the Poles the opportunity to realize both the Piast and Jagiellonian conceptions. Immediately after the cessation of hostilities Poland, in order to forestall the decisions of the Peace Conference, began to conquer neighboring territories without regard to the wishes of other nationalities and to organize them according to concepts of the surviving aristocracy.[6]

As Poland continued to expand, the pro-Polish attitude of American observers in Paris began to cool. In the United States

present-day Poland, for example, deals mainly with the "reconquered Polish western lands."

4. House diary, Sept. 14, 1918, and above, p. 98.

5. On Jan. 24, 1919, Roman Dmowski lunched with Bonsal. "It seems to me," Bonsal wrote, "that the nation he envisages is the old Poland with its manor farms stretching from the Baltic to the Black Sea—owned by gallant knights and beautiful ladies who travel to Cannes in winter and to Baden-Baden in summer. Who have expensive tastes that make it necessary for their serfs at home to work hard—very hard indeed." Stephen Bonsal, *Suitors and Suppliants*, p. 123.

6. "The aristocratic and cultured ruling classes," wrote Ginzburg, "have organized the new state under a philosophic conception of things remote from the normal realities of life. They have begun with a romantic and idealistic notion of the Polish nationality, and the desire to return to historic medievalism. . . . So immersed are the Poles in their romantic historical speculations that they do not realize that the controlling factor in the creation of a strong Poland was not the righting of historical wrongs, but the estimated service to Allied policy. . . ." Benjamin Ginzburg, "The Tragedy That Is Poland," *Nation, 111* (1920), 65–6.

the secretary of war became deeply concerned lest Polish troops enlisted in the United States had been used in the Polish hostilities against friendly nations. He suggested that the United States should refuse to permit any further enlistments and asked the secretary of state to take the matter up with the president.[7] The president on January 9, 1919, ordered immediate action to end the Polish enlistments in the United States. To Secretary Lansing Wilson wrote: "Is there not in Paris some representative of the Polish Committee with whom you could have a frank talk about this. It is clearly out of the question to allow Poles to be enlisted in the United States to fight against peoples with whom the United States is at peace and whose affairs the United States is trying to compose, but I think the representatives of the Poles should be told this before we take official action." [8] On January 23 the Polish National Committee informed the American Government that they were instructing their representatives in the United States to discontinue at once all recruiting for the Polish Army.[9]

The official attitude of the American delegation in Paris did not change in the face of continued Polish aggression. Although Wilson's pro-Polish policy considerably diminished as a result of Polish attacks and imperialistic utterances, Colonel House and other pro-Polish advisers continued to have an important influence over him.

The importance of House's position in the Polish matter was clearly recognized by Charles Seymour:

> To House were sent many appeals for assistance from struggling nationalities, not merely for decision as to ultimate

7. Acting secretary of state to the Commission to Negotiate Peace, Washington, Jan. 3, 1919, *FR: Paris Peace Conference, 1919, 2,* 424.

On Jan. 5, 1919, the secretary of state wrote the following letter to the president: "I call your attention to this telegram in regard to the enlistment of Poles in the United States.

"There are two sides to the question. The armistice does not end the state of war and I believe that the Poles would resent a change of policy at this time. On the other hand, the cessation of actual hostilities is a good excuse to stop enlistments, if it seems advisable to do so.

"Will you be good enough to indicate what reply you desire to make to the request of the Secretary of War for instructions?" Lansing to Wilson, Paris, Jan. 6, 1919, *ibid.,* pp. 425–6.

8. Wilson to Lansing, Paris, Jan. 9, 1919, *ibid.,* p. 430. Notice that this matter was not directed to Pilsudski, the head of the Polish Government, but to Dmowski, president of the Polish National Committee.

9. The chief of the Military Department of the Polish National Committee (Wielozieyski) to the American chargé in France (Bliss), Paris, Jan. 25, 1919, *ibid.,* p. 434.

boundaries, but for practical aid in the efforts they were making to establish an independent position. The most striking was
Paderewski. . . . Colonel House had for Paderewski an enduring affection which led to a friendship that after the Peace
Conference brought the two together at every opportunity.
. . . Upon President Wilson House urged the formal recognition of the Polish State and the speedy rendering of whatever
immediate assistance the Allies at Paris could furnish in a practical sense.[10]

Now that Polish recruiting in the United States had stopped,
an aggressive new Poland needed troops, arms, and ammunition.
The man who was responsible for Poland's getting them was Wilson, the miracle man of the West.

Paderewski wrote to House on January 12, 1919, pleading for
"some artillery and plenty of German-rifle munitions" with which
to protect Poland from "the murderous Ukrainian Bolshevik
army." Through this letter, in which he falsified facts, utilized the
fear of the Bolsheviks, and discredited Pilsudski's government, he
was able to influence American policy toward Poland. Because of
its importance the letter is quoted in full:

Dear Mr. House:

I have telegraphed you several times, but evidently not
one of my messages has reached you.

The American Food Commission is going to leave Warsaw
to-night. My time is very limited and, to my deepest regret, I
shall not be able to fully describe you the situation which is
simply tragic. Mr. J. M. Horodyski will give you the details. I
wish, however, to add a few remarks to his verbal report, which
will be, I am sure, very exact.

Contrary to the rumors originated by the retiring pro-
German propaganda the Poles have been nowhere the aggressive party.[11] Though claiming, most legitimately, . . . Danzig as an indispensable condition for their political, commercial, and economic life, they all rely with unshaken confidence

10. Seymour, *Intimate Papers, 4,* 261.
11. Germany was not the only country to manufacture false propaganda. "It is
fairly evident," wrote Dresel to Polk, "that the Poles are continuing the manufacture
for propaganda purposes of documents, which they pursued with great ingenuity
while the war lasted. . . . The American Legation at Warsaw confirms the view
that many of these papers are manufactured." Dresel to Polk, Aug. 5, 1919, Polk
Papers, House MSS.

on the results of the Peace Conference and do not intend to
surprise the delegates by any "fait accompli." [12] But could anybody ask them to remain quiet when brutally attacked and not
to defend themselves? Surprised by the murderous Ukrainian
Bolshevik army the women and children of Lemberg took up
arms and defended the city.[13] At the present moment a force
of about 80,000 Ukrainians, armed and equipped by the Germans, led by German and Austrian officers under the command
of an Austrian Archduke Wilhelm of Hapsburg, is at the gate
of Lemberg and the number of Polish soldiers, lacking food
and munitions, does not exceed 18,000 men. In Posen, the day
after my arrival, during the procession of 10,000 school children marching through the streets, some Prussian companies,
mostly officers, opened fire upon the peaceful and unarmed
crowd. Quite a number of shots were fired at my windows, some
of them at the window of Colonel Wade.[14] Explosive and dum-
dum bullets were used. American and British flags were insulted. Several eye-witnesses, including the officers of the
British Mission and myself, can testify to these facts.

There is no doubt that the whole affair was organized by
the Germans in order to create some new difficulties for the
Peace Conference. There is also not the slightest doubt that
the present Spartacus movement in Germany and the Bolshevik revolution in Russia are most closely connected. They
simply intend to meet on our soil.[15]

The Bolshevik army has already taken Vilna. The cities of
Grodno and Biolystok are in immediate danger. In a few days
the invasion of this part of Poland will be an accomplished
fact.[16]

Poland cannot defend itself. We have no food, no uniforms,
no arms, no munitions. We have but men, at best 500,000 of
them, willing to fight, to defend the country under a strong
Government. The present Government is weak and dangerous,
it is almost exclusively radical-socialist.[17]

12. A few weeks later the Poles did surprise the Allies with a *fait accompli.*

13. It was Poland and not Ukraine that attacked first. See Lloyd George,
Memoirs, 1, 224–5.

14. The men who fired at Paderewski were not only Germans; many of them
were Poles.

15. Paderewski is exploiting here the Bolshevik bogey.

16. The Bolsheviks did not take Vilna. It was an indigenous Polish Socialist
group that took this city.

17. Paderewski is discrediting the Polish Government in order to strengthen
the position of the Polish National Committee in Paris.

I have been asked to form a new cabinet, but what could I do with the moral support of the country alone, without the material assistance of the Allies and the United States? [18]

If there were any possibility of obtaining immediate help for my country I would suggest:

(1) To send a collective note to the Ukrainian Directorate at Kief, addressed to Messrs. Petlura, Winnitchenko, and Schwetz, ordering cessation of hostilities in Eastern Galicia and evacuation of the district of Boryslav, where considerable American, English, and French interests are endangered. [19]

(2) To send an interallied military Commission to Warsaw in order to examine the situation and prescribe the means of assistance. [20]

(3) To send as soon as possible some artillery and plenty of German rifle-munitions.

If this action is delayed our entire civilization may cease to exist. The war may only result in the establishment of barbarism all over Europe. [21]

Kindly forgive this chaotic writing.

With very kindest regards I beg to remain most gratefully and sincerely yours,

I. J. Paderewski [22]

Immediately upon receiving this letter Colonel House sent a copy of it to Wilson. In an accompanying note he stated that Paderewski's requests were moderate and urged the president to accede to his wishes and send arms, munitions and military supplies. "Now that Paderewski has formed a government in Poland which is apparently being supported by Pilsudski and the other prominent leaders, I suggest that you, on behalf of the United States, immediately recognize this Government as a *de facto* Government. I believe that we should take the lead in this matter. . . ." [23] A few days later the colonel wrote again to Wilson: "Russia must

18. Here Paderewski flatters with the admission that his power depended on American friendship.

19. It is difficult to believe that there were considerable American interests in that region.

20. When the inter-Allied military commission arrived in Warsaw and ordered the Poles to enter into truce negotiations with the Ukrainians, Poland refused.

21. "The Galician problem gave us no end of trouble," Lloyd George wrote. "The trouble, however, did not come from Bolsheviks but from Polish aggression." Lloyd George, *Memoirs, 1*, 224–5.

22. Paderewski to House, Jan. 12, 1919, House MSS. See also Seymour, *Intimate Papers, 4*, 262–4.

23. Seymour, *Intimate Papers, 4*, 264.

save herself. If she is saved by outside intervention she is not really saved. We are bound to give moral, material, and if necessary military support to protect Poland, Finland, and other such states against Bolshevik invasion." [24]

Within a few days Wilson acted upon the letter. On January 21, 1919, according to Lloyd George, President Wilson read a letter addressed to him (sic) by Paderewski.[25] In the discussion that followed the reading it was decided to appoint an inter-Allied mission to Poland to investigate and report on the situation. The Supreme Council also arranged to transport General Haller's army in France across Germany. Thus reinforced, the Poles, in spite of their promise to Wilson not to use the army for aggressive purposes, defeated the Ukrainians in Eastern Galicia, which Poland was later authorized to occupy.[26]

The question of transporting the army to Poland not only gave rise to dissensions among the Allies themselves but led to complications with Germany.[27] The Polish National Committee ardently favored moving the army; Pilsudski, fearing its use against him, was dubious.[28] The Allies finally decided to ask Germany's consent to transporting Haller's army via Danzig to Poland.[29] But Germany categorically refused and would not yield to diplomatic pressure.[30] Finally, chiefly through American and French insistence and House's influence,[31] a compromise was arranged, and the troops were taken by train through Germany to Poland. The army, ready for war upon arrival, immediately marched into Galicia, ostensibly to drive off the Bolsheviks but in reality to conquer the country and annex it to Poland. When the Supreme Council learned that Haller had invaded Galicia, it sent a message ordering him to withdraw. General Haller pretended not to have received the telegram in time to act upon its instructions.[32]

24. *Ibid.*, p. 348.
25. Lloyd George, *Memoirs, 1,* 224–5. The letter was addressed to House.
26. Seymour, *Intimate Papers, 4,* 264. See also *FR: Paris Peace Conference, 1919, 3,* 642, 671–5, 685.
27. Erzberger to the Allied Armistice Commission, Feb. 14, 1919. *FR: Paris Peace Conference, 1919, 4,* 39.
28. *Ibid., 3,* 773.
29. *Ibid., 4,* 104–7, 425–6, 472, 765.
30. *Ibid., 5,* 14, 40, 152.
31. Howard, *Theatre of Life,* p. 105. See also Paderewski to House, Mar. 7, 1919, Wiseman papers, House MSS.
32. *FR: Paris Peace Conference, 1919, 6,* 60, 191–201.

Having failed to stop Haller, the Supreme Council next tried to bring about a settlement of the dispute between Poles and Ukrainians by bringing their representatives together. The Ukrainians accepted, but the Poles declined on the ground that the security of Poland from Bolshevist attack could not be assured without the military occupation of Eastern Galicia. When the Supreme Council learned of the Polish refusal, it immediately telegraphed (March 27) Pilsudski that if Poland refused to accept the decisions of the Council the Allied and Associated Powers would no longer be justified in furnishing Poland with supplies or assistance.[33] Pilsudski refused to be intimidated. He replied that the reason for the Polish action was fear of a combined attack by the Bolsheviks and Germans, in case the treaty was not accepted. General Haller's fait accompli and Pilsudksi's refusal greatly disturbed the Allied leaders. Wilson himself was shocked, but, as Lloyd George wrote: "President Wilson was not over-anxious to offend his Polish friends by pressing the enquiry too insistently." [34]

The result of this unilateral action was that in spite of the warnings of the Western Powers and the appeals of the Galicians themselves to the Council of the Powers, the Polish Government occupied the whole of Eastern Galicia.[35] The Western Powers accepted the fact on June 25, 1919. *De jure* recognition, however, did not follow until March 1923, when the Conference of Ambassadors finally assigned Eastern Galicia to Poland.

Two powerful factors encouraged Poland's early aggression. In the first place, a greater Poland suited French policy, and the greater the better. French foreign policy was swayed by one paramount aim: the weakening of Germany and the strengthening of France's potential friends. A Polish victory offered France a supreme opportunity for achieving that end. This fact accounts for her strong desire to sever the whole of Silesia from Germany for

33. The telegram read: "The Council of the Principal Allied and Associated Powers feel that it is their duty to call the attention of the Government of Poland to facts which are giving them the greatest concern and which may lead to consequences for Poland which the Council would deeply deplore. The boundary between Poland and the Ukraine is under consideration and is as yet undetermined, and the Council has more than once informed the Polish Government that they would regard any attempt either by Poland or by the Ukrainian authorities to determine it, or to prejudice its determination, by the use of force, as a violation of the whole spirit and an arbitrary interference with the whole purpose of the present Conference of Peace, to which Poland, at least, has consented to leave the decision of questions of that sort." *FR: Paris Peace Conference, 1919, 6,* 61.

34. Lloyd George, *Memoirs, 1,* 204.

35. See *FR: Paris Peace Conference, 1919, 5,* 711–12, 754–5, 778–9, 783, 802, 806.

Poland's benefit (as well as the territories on the left bank of the Rhine for herself) without regard to ethnological or democratic considerations. France therefore encouraged the creation of a powerful Polish state which, if helped to German territories, would not only owe its security and independence to France but also play an important role in French military strategy. "A few million men—Ukrainians, Lithuanians, and White Russians—incorporated into Poland," Lloyd George wrote, "meant so much more strength added to the Eastern frontiers of France." [36]

The second factor favoring Polish aggression was the hold which the Poles had on the American delegation.[37] Wilson, it is true, came to Europe as an "enthusiastic pro-Pole," but as soon as he learned of the reckless way the Poles "trampled on his principles" he remonstrated with them. His awakening came too late. Poland, encouraged by the French and by the pro-Polish American delegation, turned deaf ears to these expostulations. In the end their defiance triumphed, and Wilson's political philosophy ended in ruin. The Poles and the French, understanding Wilson's predilections and weaknesses, took full advantage of them. "The cynicism of French diplomacy," Lloyd George stated, "was never more apparent than in its dealings with Polish delinquencies." [38]

36. Lloyd George, *Memoirs, 1,* 203.
37. According to Lloyd George the American delegation was pro-Polish because of the "existence of a powerful Polish vote in the United States." *Ibid.*
38. *Ibid., 1,* 204.

11. Poland at the Peace Conference

*Poland was an historic failure,
and always would be a failure,
and in this Treaty we were
trying to reverse the verdict
of history.*[1]

Jan Christian Smuts

THE PEACE SETTLEMENT meant the bringing of freedom to Poles, Czechs, Finns, and other nationalities. It was no simple task to determine the borders of a new state. Fully two months separated the Armistice from the inauguration of the Peace Conference on January 18, 1919. The delay adversely influenced the Senate of the United States. A simpler preliminary treaty would perhaps have commended itself to Americans eager for peace and reconstruction. Instead, the hopes of Wilson, chief of the American Democratic party, to involve his country in settlement of all the selfish broils of Europe shocked and infuriated a large segment of the American public. To Poland, on the other hand, every day's delay brought gain. The chaos resulting from three astounding events—the overturn of the Russian Government by bolshevism, and the defeat of both Germany and Austria by the Allies—gave Poland the opportunity to expand eastward, almost without restriction. Moreover, the chaos that followed the Armistice made it possible for Pilsudski to take decisive steps toward the realization of his Jagiellonian conception, while Premier and Foreign Minister Paderewski prepared himself to claim Piast Poland for his country at the Peace Conference. Widespread unemployment helped recruiting. Poland was aided by the times. Every week, indeed, gave her a larger army and a wider frontier. And with bolshevism infecting regions outside Russia, Poland was thought of as a necessary bulwark of Central Europe.

The question of Polish boundaries presented one of the greatest difficulties to the statesmen of the Peace Conference. The difficulty of applying Wilson's principle of nationality or self-determination was increased in Poland's case. The country's ethnic boundaries fluctuated from one generation to another and, in the

1. Lloyd George, *Memoirs, 1,* 465.

course of time, left large areas where the population was Polish neither by "race" nor by language. Resurrected memories of a greater Poland, now heightened by the flood of books and periodicals which reminded the statesmen of Poland's ancient glory and of the crime of crippling partitions, made it difficult for those who sought to settle national boundaries on ethnological and traditional principles. "When the Poles," Lloyd George recalled, "presented their case to the Conference, their claims were by every canon of self-determination extravagant and inadmissible." [2]

The thirteenth of the Fourteen Points declared that "an independent Polish State should be erected, which should include the territories inhabited by indisputably Polish populations, which should be assured a free and secure access to the sea. . . ." Germany had accepted the point. Indeed Germany's own claim for ethnic integrity was based on the very principle which reestablished the Polish state.

To determine and draw up frontiers between Germany and Poland in accordance with point thirteen was an enormous task. No physical barrier separated Warsaw from Berlin. Along this stretch of territory the population was mixed in varying proportions. In the partitioned and conquered areas German industrialism and culture had made an overwhelming impression on the Poles. In other areas long possessed by Germany the Poles, although retaining their native speech, were more German than Polish. Germany claimed that most of the territory was rightly hers, whereas Poland insisted that it was stolen from her inheritance and demanded its return. It was the task of the Peace Conference, of the Polish commission, and finally of the Big Three to draw the line. Between January 12 and March 14 this great work was accomplished.

The Peace Conference concerned itself primarily with the problems of the western borders of the new Poland, from East Prussia in the north to Silesia in the south—the territorial areas of the adherents of the Piast program. The eastern territories, the ambition of the Jagiellonians, lay wide open to Polish forces by reason of the disintegration of the Russian Empire and the fear of bolshevism.

The most vigorous Polish claims concerned East Prussia. It is true that the Hohenzollerns from 1525 to the Peace of Oliva

2. *Ibid.*, 2, 631.

(1660) had recognized Polish feudal overlordships over East Prussia. Before the Hohenzollerns the Grand Masters of the Teutonic Knights who controlled the region had been vassals of the Polish crown. But the Germans also had a valid historical claim, based on almost unbroken possession of the territory since 1660. During this long period it had become a primarily German land whose population was animated by an intenser nationalism than any other peoples of Germany. The Poles refused to acknowledge any German historic title to East Prussia. They vowed that their rights automatically took precedence over the German, and therefore demanded large portions of East Prussia and a wider corridor to the sea, as well as the German-inhabited port of Danzig.

The Piast conception was evoked to afford a motive not only for the Polish yearning for the sea but also for an active policy on the southwest border of Poland, in Silesia. The history of Silesia is neither German nor Polish. It is the history of Germans and Poles. In this area the two peoples came into closest contact. Silesia once belonged to the historic empire of the Piasts. But when after 170 years of rule in Poland the Piast dynasty split up the country into various duchies, Silesia too was divided. One of the first partitions of Silesia (1163) marks the beginning of its Germanization. The lack of any central power in Poland forced the Silesian princes to act on their own and, for obvious geographical reasons, to fall more and more under German influence. As centuries went by, the Silesian Piasts, submitting to Germanization, finally abandoned their own people and became Germans.

Upper Silesia never came ethnically to be a German country in the same sense as Lower Silesia. The majority of the inhabitants of the rural areas spoke Polish and heard mass in Polish; the towns remained predominantly German. But language alone is no test of nationality. It does not reveal national sentiment or mirror the political desires of the people. Nor is religion proof of nationalism.

The Poles it is true, were devout Catholics; their common allegiance to the Roman Catholic Church formed a bond between Russian and German Poles in the years following the partitions. This bond was perhaps stronger than ties of language and tradition. Yet how much of this was genuine nationalism and how much was merely opposition to Protestant Germany and Greek-Orthodox Russia is not so easy to determine. The Polish clergy and the Polish agitators made the most of the opportunity offered them by the

collapse of Germany and Russia to claim that what was Catholic
must be Polish and what was Polish must be Catholic.[3]

In one part of Upper Silesia (Austrian Silesia) the people considered themselves "Silesians" and preferred "Austrian Catholi-
cism." [4] Although they spoke Polish, their cultural preference was
German. In the western parts of the area many of the "Silesians"
were attracted by Czech culture. Rich landowners disregarded
their national fate; miners wanted union with Germany; some
farmers showed a desire to unite with Poland; and many others
wanted neither Berlin nor Warsaw to control their affairs.

When the time came for the Peace Conference to open, both
the adherents of Pilsudski and the followers of Dmowski were
ready with their territorial claims, which, if granted, would have
made Poland one of the largest states in Europe. It was extremely
difficult, however, for these two antagonistic forces to choose one
delegation to represent them. The man who helped give Poland
one voice at the conference was Colonel House, avowed friend of
Poland, influential member of the American delegation, and powerful confidant of President Wilson.

For many days before the conference convened Colonel House's
office was deluged with Polish delegations. "They have come,"
Bonsal recorded, "in ever-increasing numbers not only from Cracow and Chicago, where Poles thrive, but they have come from all
the four corners of the earth." Each declared himself to be the
only committee duly authorized to represent *Polonia restituta.*
Every delegation demanded precedence and priority. Some ac-
claimed Paderewski; others hailed Pilsudski. All of them apparently sensed that their recognition as well as the Allied acquiescence in Polish territorial claims depended principally on the
American delegation.

Colonel House after surveying the chaotic situation (January
5, 1919) decided to intervene. He ordered Bonsal to summon all
the Poles to his office and deliver, in his name, an ultimatum that
Poland would be allotted only two delegates. "There must be no
more of the *liberum veto,*" House told Bonsal, "which, as all historians agree, killed independent Poland in other days. If an

3. For an excellent analysis of this problem see Frederick W. Kaltenbach, *Self-
Determination, 1919* (London, 1938), especially pp. 34–5.
4. When this fact came up at the Peace Conference, Paderewski blamed the
Catholic Austrian clergy for the lack of Polish nationalism in that area. And for
this reason the new Polish premier requested that no plebiscite should be held there.
See *FR: Paris Peace Conference, 1919, 6,* 191–201, and below, pp. 133–4.

agreement cannot be reached, then Poland cannot be represented in the Congress of Nations, which would be too bad." [5] In less than two weeks Paderewski and Dmowski became the official delegates of Poland, while Dluski, Pilsudski's choice, was merely an alternate.

The Americans came to the Peace Conference better supplied with documents than anyone else.[6] The members of the Inquiry, already referred to, were in Paris from December 1918 on, forming there the Intelligence Section of the American delegation. By January 22, 1919, three days after the official opening of the Peace Conference, the American plenipotentiaries already had a document of importance, the *Outline of Tentative Report* on the frontiers of Europe.[7]

The authors of the *Tentative Report* recommended that Poland be given "a secure and unhampered access to the Baltic." They supported this conclusion with the following argument:

> The problem of Poland's access to the sea is very difficult. If such access is accorded through continuous Polish territory the province of East Prussia, with a population of 1,600,000 Germans will be cut off from the rest of Germany. If Poland does not thus secure access to the sea, 600,000 Poles in West Prussia [Pomorze] will remain under German rule and 20,000,000 Poles in Poland proper will probably have but a hampered and precarious commercial outlet, subject to alien . . . and hostile decision.

They therefore recommended that the "corridor" and Danzig be ceded to Poland. As far as East Prussia was concerned, they believed that although it would be territorially cut off from the rest of Germany, it could "easily be assured railroad transit across the Polish corridor." This, they argued, was a simple matter compared with assuring port facilities to Poland. "In the case of Poland," the report reads, "they are vital interests; in the case of Germany, aside from Prussian sentiment, they are quite secondary."

Not until February 25, 1919, did Colonel House order the Intelligence Section to submit the final report on the *Proposed*

5. Bonsal, *Suitors and Suppliants,* pp. 118–20.

6. See Nicolson, *Peacemaking,* p. 28.

7. David Hunter Miller, *My Diary at the Peace Conference of Paris* (privately printed, 1924), *6,* 43 ff.

New Boundaries for Germany.[8] In it Lord and Bowman suggested that on the west the Polish-German frontier should follow the "linguistic frontier as closely as topography and some peculiarities of the railways system permit." They assigned Danzig to Poland, while the southern belt of East Prussia, known as Mazuria, was given the right to hold a referendum to determine whether the inhabitants preferred to remain in Germany or be united to Poland.

In explanatory remarks the authors of the *New Boundaries* report insisted on the necessity of giving Poland a secure territorial access to the sea: "Any other arrangement would be awkward and precarious." With regard to Danzig the American experts wrote:

> Danzig is to-day unquestionably a German city. . . . It is incontestable, however, that Danzig owed its own importance in the past to its position as the natural port of the great Polish hinterland behind it, and that if the principle of the Polish corridor to the sea is accepted at all, it must almost inevitably involve the great port at the mouth of the Vistula. . . . Furthermore, the creation of another Polish port alongside it would probably leave Danzig condemned to utter stagnation.[9]

At the preliminary meeting of the Peace Conference on January 18, 1919, a territorial commission was set up to examine Polish claims. Before giving the Polish commission its instructions it was decided to invite Roman Dmowski to appear before the Council of Ten to present the case of Poland. On January 29 Dmowski spoke for some five hours to the Allied leaders, using French and English alternately. His address was aimed primarily at winning the sympathy of Wilson.[10] He suggested that in determining the territory to belong to Poland the Council of Ten should start with the year 1772, before the first partition. He warned that the principle of including within the boundaries only those territories where the Poles were in a large majority must not be accepted altogether. In the west Poland could not be satisfied with

8. *Ibid.* (*Proposed New Boundaries for Germany. Prepared by American Intelligence Section, February 25, 1919.*)

9. The American experts were quite wrong in declaring that another port would cause the decline of Danzig. The interwar period showed that the great Polish port of Gdynia, only 12 miles from Danzig, did not reduce the importance of Danzig at all.

10. W. F. Reddaway, "The Peace Conference," in Reddaway, *Cambridge History of Poland*, p. 496. See also *FR: Paris Peace Conference, 3,* 772-84.

the historical boundaries of 1772. Dmowski wanted Silesia, which was lost to Poland in the 14th century, as well as Danzig which Poland lost in 1743. He also desired large parts of East Prussia. Dmowski, Lloyd George recorded, "made no secret of the rejection by the Poles of the application to some of their claims of the principle of self-determination: 'In settling the boundaries of Poland the principle . . . must not be accepted altogether.' " [11] On February 26 the Supreme Council asked the Commission on Polish Affairs to submit their report by March 8.

The commission lost no time. Its subcommission, composed of General Le Rond, Isaiah Bowman, and Lieutenant Colonel Kisch, worked unceasingly. Their primary concern was the western frontiers of Poland. On March 6 the plan of their report was sent to Jules Cambon, chairman of the commission. On the same day the full commission gave a long hearing to Dmowski. On March 7 and 9 it held two sessions for a final revision of its report. On March 12 the text was delivered to the Supreme Council.[12]

Six general principles guided the deliberations of the experts in establishing the frontiers between Poland and Germany. The first stated that "primary consideration [should] be given to the line of ethnic separation in such a way as to secure the fairest possible settlement between the two peoples concerned," and the second that rectification of the frontier, in some places in favor of the Germans, ought to be made where the ethnic facts were outweighed by the other facts and principles involved. Third, due weight was to be attached to lines of religious cleavage, as, for example, in Mazuria, where the population was Protestant although its speech was akin to Polish. Fourth, slight adjustments should be made in a line based on the above determining considerations wherever such adjustments would make the proposed line coincide with "a well-recognized line of historical division," as, for example, on the borders of the province of Poznania, which coincided with the frontier of the kingdom of Poland prior to 1772. Fifth, economic relations and existing means of communication should be taken into consideration so that the normal industrial life of each community might be restored as quickly as possible. Sixth, account should be taken of the exposed situation of Poland between Russia on the one hand and Germany on the other, and after all the above factors had been duly studied attention should be paid to strengthening

11. Lloyd George, *Memoirs, 1*, 204–5.
12. *FR: Paris Peace Conference, 1919, 4*, 624.

the defensive frontiers of the new Polish state: "While such a strengthening in no case gives Poland any advantage for offensive action, it diminishes to some extent the dangers which threaten her, exposed as she is to attack on the east, the west and the north, over unobstructed plains which offer at best but insignificant natural defenses."

According to these principles the commission recommended a frontier between Germany and Poland based on a variety of territorial, historical, strategic, and linguistic considerations. After they had finished their report, little was left of Wilson's principle of nationality.

Although the Supreme Council had asked the commission to finish its report by March 8, it was not until March 19 that the council opened its discussion. At once Mr. Lloyd George stigmatized the report as unjust. He noted that the number of Germans to be included in the future Polish state as drawn up by the commission was not less than 2,132,000. He considered that a large figure which might spell serious trouble for Poland in the future:

> I was as sincere an advocate of Polish independence as any member of the Commission, but I was convinced that to add to Poland populations which would be an alien and hostile element inside its boundaries would be a source of permanent weakness and danger and not of strength to this resurrected State. I knew that a time would come when Germany would respond to the cry of its exiled people and restore them to the Fatherland by force of arms.
>
> For that reason I renewed my pressure in the Conference to reject the recommendations which incorporated in Poland towns and territories which were overwhelmingly German by language, race and inclination. . . .
>
> President Wilson was uneasy at the arguments advanced against the conclusions of the Polish Commission. His experts failed to remove his misgivings.[13]

Lloyd George also feared that the Germans might hesitate to sign a treaty containing such a provision. He further remarked that the Poles had no high reputation as administrators. He therefore asked the committee to restrict the Polish claims so as to diminish the German population assigned to Poland. It was most unwise, he warned, to assign 412,000 Germans in the Danzig dis-

13. Lloyd George, *Memoirs, 2*, 643.

trict alone. Lloyd George based his stand on the simple proposition that he "did not want any more Alsace-Lorraines in Europe, whether in the East or the West."

Colonel House was the first to answer Lloyd George's attack. He said that the American delegates were convinced that Danzig should go to Poland, and he expected the British delegates eventually to agree. He suggested that the problem of an East Prussian island could readily be solved either by internationalization or by converting it into a separate republic. Clemenceau supported House, Lloyd George observed, in a highly characteristic remark which summed up centuries of French policy: "the more separate and independent republics were established in Germany the better he would be pleased." [14]

President Wilson felt the same anxieties as Prime·Minister Lloyd George. He said he was aware that the Germans might someday yearn to rescue German populations from Polish rule and that this desire would be hard to resist. There was bound to be a mixture of hostile populations included in either state. The Supreme Council would have to decide which mixture promised the best prospect of security. It was a question of balancing antagonistic considerations. [15]

Cambon declared Poland's free access to the sea to be essential. He thought a large proportion of the German population would emigrate to other parts of Germany when the Polish state was constituted. Cambon and Clemenceau were supported by the American experts who, according to Lloyd George, "were fanatical pro-Poles, and their judgment in any dispute in which Poland was concerned was vitiated by an invincible partnership. There was therefore no hope of redress in a reference back to the Commission." [16] Nevertheless, it was agreed to refer the report on the boundaries of Poland back to the commission in the light of the foregoing discussion.

On March 20 the Cambon commission reassembled, but it did not modify its previous decisions. The commission now voted unanimously in favor of the text of a note sent on the same day to the Supreme Council, in which its original recommendations were maintained without exception. [17]

14. *Ibid.*, *1*, 188–9.
15. *FR: Paris Peace Conference, 1919, 4,* 418.
16. Lloyd George, *Memoirs, 2,* 643.
17. *FR: Paris Peace Conference, 1919, 4,* 449.

The council again discussed the question in its session of March 22.[18] Lloyd George was alarmed by the effect the report would produce; the commission was giving too large a German population away to Poland. Once more he expressed his fear that Germany would not sign the treaty.[19] He was inclined, however, to accept provisionally the solution proposed by the commission, reserving to the Supreme Council the right of revision.

Wilson agreed with the procedure in general, but raised the question how the public could be made to understand that the council's acceptance of these frontiers for Poland was provisional. After a short discussion, a formula proposed by Wilson was adopted by which "the new report of the Commission on Polish Affairs was received and discussed and reserved for final examination in connection with subsequent boundary determination affecting Germany."

Lloyd George, having lost faith in the procedures of the council, acted on his own. When "the controversy was at its greatest intensity" he sent the famous Fontainebleau memorandum (March 25, 1919) to his colleagues on the council.[20] In this document he fully explained his fears. He pointed out that the Peace Conference would of necessity be "severe, hard, and even merciless," but that it should at the same time be so just that no country should feel deprived of the right to complain.[21] In substance, the memorandum was an appeal to France for moderation of its traditional policy of disrupting and dismembering the German Reich, in the interests of a lasting peace and a European organization secure against bolshevism.[22] Specifically, it attacked French proposals for the Saar, the Rhineland, and Poland, as "unwarranted and dangerous violations of the principle of nationality likely to result in future wars." It played on the present danger of bolshevism, reciting the news of Bela Kun in Hungary and the continued activities of the Spartacists in Germany, and predicted that all of Eastern Europe would be swept into the orbit of bolshevism. "The greatest danger that I see in the present situation," Lloyd George warned,

> is that Germany may throw in her lot with Bolshevism and place her resources, her brains, her vast organizing power at

18. *Ibid.*
19. *Ibid., 4,* 449–50.
20. Lloyd George, *Memoirs, 2,* 643; *1,* 266–73.
21. Temperley, *A History of the Peace Conference, 6,* 545–6.
22. The French reply stated that if Lloyd George feared bolshevism he should build up Poland as a strong barrier. Lloyd George, *Memoirs, 1,* 273–6.

the disposal of the revolutionary fanatics whose dream it is to conquer the world for Bolshevism by force of arms.[23]

The proposal of the Polish Commission that we should place 2,100,000 Germans under the control of a people which is of a different religion and which has never proved its capacity for stable self-government throughout its history must, in my judgment, lead sooner or later to a new war in the East of Europe.[24]

Before finally settling the issue of Danzig, the corridor, and Upper Silesia, the Council of Four decided to invite Paderewski to appear before them to present the Polish case against modification of the commission's report. Paderewski saw the British prime minister first, but Lloyd George refused to change his mind. The Pole's brief appearance before the council did not result in any essential gains for Poland. Wilson, as was his wont, sent Paderewski a billet-doux designed to assuage his wounded feelings. He wrote, in the name of the Supreme Council:

> Before you leave Paris I would like to express our appreciation for the help you have given in aiding us to reach decisions in the difficult and delicate questions which have arisen regarding Poland and her neighbors.
>
> Your grasp of the various problems, your keen insight into the historic and ethnic relations governing that part of Europe, and your willingness to accept a broad rather than a narrow basis of settlement has impressed us all. I speak of my colleagues as well as myself when I say that your attitude has given us confidence that Poland will soon again take her place among the potential powers, and become an influence toward the political liberty and advancement of mankind.[25]

By April 5 Wilson and Lloyd George were in full agreement that the city and area of Danzig must become a free city with full local autonomy under a League of Nations commissioner. The status of Danzig was a major test of Wilson's principles.[26] "Mezes had seen the President," Miller noted in his *Diary*, "and it appears that Lloyd George was opposed to giving Danzig to the Poles, and the president agreed to this because he did not want Fiume to go to the Italians, and if Danzig went to the Poles he would have to

23. Lloyd George, *Memoirs, 1,* 268.
24. *Ibid., 1,* 267.
25. Wilson to Paderewski, Apr. 26, 1919, Wilson MSS.
26. Paul Birdsall, *Versailles Twenty Years After* (New York, 1941), p. 178.

consent to Fiume being Italian. So in his talk with Mezes he said that Danzig and the area around it was to be either free or international or independent." [27] Wilson's bias in favor of Poland seems to have been counterbalanced by his prejudice against the Italians. "Cynics pointed to the fact," Churchill wrote, "that Italian emigrants to America usually return to Italy without acquiring voting rights, while the Polish vote was a formidable factor in the domestic politics of the United States." [28]

The final arrangements profoundly changed the recommendations of the Commission on Polish Affairs. Danzig was placed under international control, whereas Upper Silesia was awarded to Poland. It was decided to hold a plebiscite over Marienwerder; and when that was carried out, on March 29, 1920, the districts of Allenstein and Marienwerder were awarded to Germany. Thus, under the influence of Lloyd George and with Wilson's belated support, the French policy of dismembering Germany was checked and the Wilsonian principles of self-determination and nationality were temporarily preserved. [29]

Compromise did not end the Polish problem. Germany protested against the award of Upper Silesia to Poland. Lloyd George and ultimately Wilson became convinced that there must be a plebiscite in that area as well. In May the Germans pointed out that the award was based on neither racial, historical, nor economic grounds. They warned the Allies that it would weaken Germany's ability to meet the reparation payments and that they were convinced it would awaken Irredentism. [30] This with certain other German complaints created consternation in the British delegation, partly because of the inherent justice of the German charge that the settlement of Upper Silesia violated the Fourteen Points, and also from fear that Germany would refuse to sign the treaty. [31]

At first Wilson believed the British concern to be motivated not by justice but by fear. He agreed to support modifications where he could be convinced that his principles had been violated. It did not take long to persuade the president that Upper Silesia was a case in point.

27. Miller, *My Diary*, 9, 208.
28. Churchill, *The Aftermath*, p. 219.
29. The same Poles who had hitherto lauded Wilson as their "savior" now began to attack him bitterly for his change of heart. See Abbé Tworkowski's polemic brochure, *Wilson et la question polonaise*.
30. *FR: Paris Peace Conference, 1919, 6*, 117 and 795.
31. *Ibid., 6*, 139–42.

It was not an easy matter for Wilson to support Lloyd George. He had to contend with his experts, chiefly with Professor Robert H. Lord, who while he insisted on the Polish character of Upper Silesia flatly opposed a plebiscite to test the accuracy of his assertion. Dr. Lord argued that a fair and free plebiscite would establish the Polish character of that area, but he denied the possibility of a really free vote under the social and economic conditions which then prevailed there.

Wilson showed the effect of Lord's argument during the meeting of the Council of Four on June 3, 1919. When Lloyd George asserted that an accurate plebiscite in Upper Silesia was possible, Wilson expressed doubt whether a free vote could be taken. Lord had informed him, he said, "that the people in Upper Silesia were entirely dominated by a small number of magnates and capitalists, not exceeding 20 all together. . . ."

Lloyd George replied that talk of intimidation had no basis in fact. In the election of 1912, he pointed out, Poles in Upper Silesia cast 97,000 votes for their representatives as against 82,000 other votes. As Wilson continued to be adamant, the British prime minister said that he stood by Wilson's Fourteen Points and "that his understanding of self-determination was that of the people themselves, not that of experts like Mr. Lord." He could not, he continued, "accept the view that any experts could judge better than the people themselves."

At the end of the discussion Wilson accepted in principle the idea of a plebiscite. Germany, he proposed, should be told that a plebiscite would be held under strict guarantees and safeguards, to be laid down by an international commission. Should she reject the condition, he added, "there will be no plebiscite." [32] On the following day the Polish commission was instructed to prepare draft articles for the plebiscite.

It was Polish Prime Minister Paderewski who finally clinched the argument. On June 5 he was invited to appear before the Supreme Council to present his views. In his introductory remarks Paderewski challenged the justice of the plebiscite. In the agricultural western part of Upper Silesia, he said, the Poles are under the domination of German Catholic clergy. The influence of that clergy "is most dangerous for us, because those people rule absolutely our people, and in the case of a plebiscite they would, even in spite of our majorities amounting in many districts to ninety

32. *Ibid., 6,* 147–55.

per cent and more . . . decidedly follow the orders of the German clergy." For this reason Paderewski insisted that a plebiscite would be "absolutely impossible." "In the eastern district, the people, of course, are free from that influence; they are more conscious of their nationality and of their political aspirations, and they would, of course, declare themselves for Poland."

Paderewski further stated that he was not concerned over the eastern part of Silesia where, according to him, the workers and miners would vote for Poland.[33] But, he explained, there would be some inconvenience in having that territory alone assigned to Poland, because it would leave the whole mining industry on the frontier and consequently accessible to invasion and destruction by gunfire. He demanded therefore that the agricultural area surrounding it be assigned to Poland. But since, he confessed, there was little racial consciousness among the Polish peasants he could not agree to a plebiscite.

In the debate that followed Paderewski's unsubstantiated claims Lloyd George showed incredulity. Paderewski, fearing defeat, told the council:

Mr. President and Gentlemen, I call your attention to the fact that the changes which you intend to introduce into the treaty might endanger the whole situation, not of my country alone, but of Eastern Europe. For the last few months Poland has been a stronghold of peace and order in the East. We have had no sign of revolution, no sign of Bolshevism, and if there is fighting, it is unfortunately fighting on the borders. It is not due to our people. It is due to the necessity of defending ourselves. We have not attacked anyone, and I am ready to prove the truth of my statement by facts at any moment.[34]

33. While visiting Upper Silesia in January 1919, Professor Archibald Coolidge of the American Commission observed the opposite. The great landowners, he informed the Commission to Negotiate Peace, were almost indifferent to their national fate. "The miners are rather in favor of continued union with Germany, believing that it will be more of their interest to be part of the German economic union than of the Polish one. The agricultural population, on the other hand, are more national in sentiment and desire union with Poland." Coolidge to Commission to Negotiate Peace, Jan. 9, 1919, *FR: Paris Peace Conference, 2,* 227–8. See also Kolarz, *Myths and Realities in Eastern Europe,* pp. 128–30.

34. This and the quotations that follow are from the Stenographic Report of a Meeting Held at President Wilson's House in the Place des États-Unis, June 5, 1919, *FR: Paris Peace Conference, 6,* 191–201.

Lloyd George immediately interrupted to remark slyly: "There was a telegram this morning which I read that you are still advancing in the Ukrainian part of Galicia."

"There is some misunderstanding," Paderewski answered,

> concerning Ukrainia and Galicia. . . . We have been asked to stop that fighting, or, to put it more clearly and precisely, I have been asked by General Bliss in behalf of you, Mr. President, to agree to an armistice, which I did in principle. . . . However decisive were our efforts, we could not keep back those boys of twenty years of age. They went on. They simply marched like a storm. . . .

"Does Poland claim the whole of Galicia?" asked the British prime minister. "Historically, yes," Paderewski answered.

> We have given autonomy to this country. We claim the whole of Galicia. We claim it for the simple reason that it is absolutely impossible to define ethnographically this country, because, curiously enough, and we should rather be proud of the fact, in the center of Galicia there is more of a Ukrainian population than on the border. The farthest districts of Galicia are more Polish than the immediate surroundings of Lemberg. There isn't a neighborhood of Lemberg which contains eighty per cent.

Before Lloyd George was able to question Paderewski's "historic" claim to the Ukraine Wilson, perhaps intentionally, changed the subject. He asked Paderewski whether he expected the agricultural communes in Upper Silesia to vote for union with Germany. Paderewski answered affirmatively. "If you took the opinion of Silesia as a whole," Lloyd George interrupted, "would it be German?" "Yes," Paderewski replied, "as a whole it would be German."

Paderewski had fallen into the trap. He immediately realized that this admission nullified his previous assertions and consequently could jeopardize Polish claims. He therefore decided to use a different approach. "If there is any change in that which has been already granted to Poland," he told the Supreme Council with dramatic emphasis,

> I should immediately resign, because I could not return to my country if there is any such change as a plebiscite here. . . .

If there are such changes, I couldn't have anything more to do with politics, because it would be absolutely impossible to rule my country. You know that revolutions begin when people lose faith in their leadership. These people have belief in me now, because they were told by me, and most emphatically, that these things promised to them would be given to them. Well now, if something is taken away from them, they will lose all faith in my leadership. They will lose faith in your leadership of humanity; and there will be revolution in my country.

This was too much for Lloyd George. In an angry outburst he declared:

Here is Poland that five years ago was torn to pieces, under the heel of three great powers, with no human prospect of recovering its liberty; certainly without the slightest chance of recovering it by its own exertions. . . . Why, during the four or five years of the war the Poles were actually fighting against their own freedom in so far as they were fighting at all. . . . She has won her freedom, not by her own exertions, but by the blood of others; and not only has she no gratitude, but she says she loses faith in the people who won her freedom.

"I am very sorry," Paderewski answered. "Perhaps I did not express myself precisely enough. If I say that I would not be able to lead these people any more because they may lose faith in my leadership, I don't mean to imply that they are losing faith in your leadership."

"I was only referring to what you said," interrupted Lloyd George. "We won freedom for nations that had not the slightest hope of it—Czechoslovakia, Poland, and others. Nations that have won their freedom at the expense of the blood of the Italians and Frenchmen and Englishmen and Americans. And we have the greatest trouble in the world to keep them from annexing other nations and imposing upon other nations the very tyranny which they have themselves endured for centuries. . . ." The case for a plebiscite was now somewhat stronger.

The Polish commission was not ready to present its draft articles for the plebiscite to the Supreme Council until June 11. The experts still opposed a plebiscite. They agreed to formulate details only under direct orders from the council. When Clemenceau asked Lloyd George if he would like to hear the report of the commission, the latter replied: "The Commission is very partial to Poland. I do not wish to discuss Poland with it." [35]

The final announcement of the decision to hold a plebiscite was made by Wilson on June 14. In doing so he showed the influence of Paderewski's admission on his own attitude. He reminded the Poles that Paderewski himself had distinguished between the industrial and agricultural zones. He assured them, however, that they would have an adequate interval to eliminate undue German influence, and promised that the plebiscite would be conducted under the impartial guard of an Allied military force.[36]

The assurance was duly honored. The promise to hold impartial voting was breached not by the Germans but by the Poles and the French troops stationed in Upper Silesia. The Allied troops which were present during the plebiscite of May 1921 were not impartial. The irregular forces of the Polish freebooter Wojciech Korfanty were allowed to roam the area without any attempt by the French troops to suppress them.[37] Yet the total vote for Upper Silesia showed a three to two majority for Germany. When the area was divided in accordance with local majorities, the western agricultural section was allotted to Germany and the smaller but wealthier industrial section in the east was given to Poland.[38]

35. Miller, *My Diary, 19,* 97–9.

36. Colonel House was disappointed at Wilson's decision. He wrote: "I am afraid it cannot be honestly carried out." Seymour, *Intimate Papers, 4,* 482.

37. See W. J. Rose, *The Drama of Upper Silesia: A Regional Study* (Brattleboro, Vt., 1935), pp. 140–41, 173–4. See also Robert Machray, *The Problem of Upper Silesia* (London, 1945), pp. 28–9.

38. The League of Nations, on the basis of "economic necessity" and not of "self-determination," decided (Oct. 12, 1920) to partition the region thus.

12. Conclusion

*If it had not been for Colonel House,
there would be no independent
Poland to-day.*[1]

Ignace J. Paderewski

ONE CANNOT BUT CONCLUDE that Woodrow Wilson's friendship for Poland was one of the important factors that led to the re-establishment of a Polish state. The president was one of the first leaders of a powerful country to champion the cause of Poland. His speech of February 1917 and his declaration of the Fourteen Points in January 1918 encouraged the Poles in Europe and in America to unite and fight more vigorously for Polish independence. Before that, as Colonel House rightly observed, they had been divided among themselves and had not even dreamt that after the war a united, free, and independent Poland might be established.

It would be a mistake to say that President Wilson was an enthusiastic pro-Pole throughout his political career. His friendship for Poland was affected by many varying and contradictory factors that resulted in changing his early uncomplimentary feeling toward Polish-Americans into a genuinely pro-Polish attitude which before long became vacillating and in the end concealed strong misgivings.

Wilson first began to take interest in Poland late in 1915, when the problem of relief aroused—and frustrated—the desire of the American people to help the starving people in Eastern Europe. Humanitarian and ethical considerations prompted the president to take vigorous action to help these unfortunates. Utilizing the power of his office, he appealed directly, without any selfish interests, to the heads of the belligerent powers to spare the civilian populations undue hardships and allow America to send them relief.

When Paderewski visited Wilson for the first time, the president was already "Polish-minded," primarily because of Colonel House's influence. It did not take long for the pianist to influence

1. Paderewski made this statement to a group of newspapermen on Jan. 23, 1919. House diary, Jan. 23, 1919. Its validity is difficult to deny after one has reviewed the history of the rebirth of Poland.

138

Wilson, this time politically, by telling him of the "shocking crime of the Polish partitions." Wilson, true product of 19th-century liberalism, was most sympathetic. To him, as to so many of the contemporary liberals who knew little of Polish political and social history, the partitions of Poland seemed an act of brigandage—an appalling legacy of the 18th century that had to be rectified.

As the presidential elections approached, Wilson's humanitarianism and liberalism became intertwined with his own political ambition. In the Polish question he saw an opportunity to use his already well-known attitude for his own benefit. Thus, up to the election he grew more openly pro-Polish, and this indirectly affected American public opinion on the Polish problem.

After the autumn of 1916 Wilson's feeling for Poland began to cool. The political pressure of American Poles under the ostensible leadership of Paderewski filled him with misgivings and distrust. He became aware of the political embarrassments of championing one minority in a country that abounded in hyphenated Americans. But it was already too late to change. For a while he did succeed in fending off some of the exaggerated demands of Paderewski's group, but in the end under the pressure of his pro-Polish advisers he played out his role as patron saint of Poland.

Wilson's awakening came during the Peace Conference. The territorial ambitions of the Poles, their open disavowal of Wilson's own principles of self-determination, their forceful incorporation of non-Polish territories, and their persecution of minorities within their own borders gave proof of the bankruptcy of his political philosophy. The president, however, was a stubborn man who did not wish to acknowledge his political mistakes. Thus in spite of disappointments and disenchantments he continued out of pride to champion the Polish cause to the bitter end.

Today, again, some Poles in exile and at home are calling upon God to grant them a universal war that will liberate Poland from the Soviet yoke. Again it is to the United States that their attention is directed, for it is only from the United States that the miracle of liberation could come. But an increasing number of Poles in America as well as Poland are becoming passive and apathetic to the plight of Poland, realizing that in this atomic age the miracle of liberation may turn out to be total destruction.

Bibliographical Essay

THE INABILITY of the Poles to preserve their political existence at the end of the 18th century, as well as the failure of the democratic experiment in reborn Poland in the first quarter of the 20th century, has had an unfortunate effect on the nature and character of Polish historiography. Self-criticism is rare. It takes place only when the authors address a Polish forum, and even then they stress the injustice of the outside world toward Poland rather than the deficiencies of Polish patriotism, sense of nationalism, and social cleavages.

The fact that Poland did not exist as a political entity throughout the latter part of the 18th century and the whole of the 19th century encouraged many Polish historians to take a defensive attitude. The unwillingness of the Poles to admit their own responsibility for the many catastrophes that have befallen their country has introduced a persistent theme in Polish historiography. Even today the essential problem in Polish historical thought is to resolve the question of the partitions and of the responsibility for them. For excellent works on Polish historiography consult Wladyslaw Smolenski's *Szkoly Historyczne* (Warsaw, 1925), and Waclaw Lednicki's *Life and Culture of Poland* (New York, 1944). The first chapter, of the latter volume, especially, analyzes Polish literature dealing with the partitions.

It is not surprising that as soon as Poland regained her independence in 1918 Polish historians and political scientists were obliged to misrepresent the contribution of indigenous and foreign Polish leaders to the resurrection of the state. To obtain a full and unbiased story of the forces that led to the rebirth of Poland it was necessary not only to examine the numerous Polish sources critically but above all to study the diplomacy of other powers during the first World War and the contribution of the Polish minority group in the United States toward a revival of Polish sovereignty. Professor C. A. Fyffe was perhaps right when he wrote that Poland had no history but only neighbors, implying that the only way to understand Polish history is to study the history of her neighbors who have shaped and still do shape her destiny.

There are but few excellent general studies of Polish history. Marjan Seyda's *Polska na Przelomie Dziejow* (Posen, 1927) is now dated. It exaggerates the Polish role in bringing about the re-establishment of Poland but is still valuable in presenting the political, intellectual, and social forces that have shaped the history of Poland. Competent works are Roman Dyboski's *Outlines of Polish History* (London, 1932) and *Poland* (New York, 1933). A general history of Poland is *The Cambridge History of Poland, 1697–1935* (Cambridge, Eng., Cambridge University Press, 1941), edited by W. F. Reddaway; but the treatment of the 1914–20 period is too sketchy to be of great value for the understanding of the forces and events that led to the rebirth of Poland. An outstanding analytical work is Henryk Frankel's *Poland: The Struggle for Power: 1772–1939* (London, 1946). For a lucid analysis of the political and social forces in Poland see Walter Kolarz's *Myths and Realities in Eastern Europe* (London, 1946). An excellent and penetrating study of Polish history is William J. Rose's *Poland, Old and New* (London, 1948).

There are some notable special studies of various phases of Polish political history in the 18th and 19th centuries. Jean Jacques Rousseau's "Considération sur le Gouvernement de Pologne (1771)," in C. E. Vaughan, ed., *The Political Writings of Jean Jacques Rousseau* (Cambridge, Eng., 1915), is a profound and realistic essay. After a careful study of the internal conditions in Poland the famous French philosopher, a year before the first partition of Poland, advised the Poles to reduce the size of their country and rid themselves of "traditions" that had made Poland impotent. A competent account of the political and social conditions in Poland during the reign of Stanislaw-August, the last king of Poland, is D. W. Kalinka's *Ostatnie Lata Panowania Stanislawa Augusta* (Cracow, 1891). R. Nisbett Bain's *The Last King of Poland and His Contemporaries* (New York, 1909) is a scholarly work which describes the anarchical conditions in Poland on the eve of the first partition.

The two standard works on the partitions of Poland are Lord Eversley's *The Partitions of Poland* (New York, 1915) and Robert H. Lord's *The Second Partition of Poland* (Cambridge, Mass., 1915). The latter is by far more the authoritative and scholarly. Both authors blame the major European powers, particularly Russia, for the partitions. Both place too much weight on the external factors which brought about the downfall of Poland. Chester V. Easum's *Prince Henry of Prussia* (University of Wisconsin Press, 1942) is a well-written and amply documented work. The author exonerates Frederick the Great of having initiated the partition of Poland and blames Catherine II for first suggesting partition. A first-rate scholarly work which analyzes the attitude of Great Britain as well as some other major powers toward the first partition is D. B. Horn's *British Public Opinion and the First Partition of Poland* (Edinburgh, 1945). The writer discloses the lack of sympathy and concern over the fate of Poland displayed by the major statesmen of the period.

Bronislaw Limanowski's *Powstanie 1863–64* (Lwow, 1892) is a very competent study of the Polish insurrection of 1863–64, which attributes its failure to lack of patriotism among the Polish people. The same author's *Historia Demokracji Polskiej* (Zurich, 1901) offers a rounded and valuable account of Polish political thought. It still remains the standard work although now dated.

Works on the Socialist movement in Poland are limited. Ignace Daszynski's *Polityka Proletariatu* (Warsaw, 1907) is useful. Although polemical it is one of the best histories of Polish socialism. It is well supplemented by the same writer's *Pamietniki* (Cracow, 1925), which is based on the personal diaries of this Socialist leader.

Those books which offer the best means of gauging the Bolshevik attitude toward the rebirth of Poland are Joseph Stalin's *Marxism and the National and Colonial Question* (New York, c. 1912), Karl Marx and Friedrich Engels' *Selected Correspondence 1846–1895* (New York, 1942), V. I. Lenin's *The Essentials of Lenin* (London, 1947), and Bertram D. Wolfe's *Three Who Made a Revolution: Lenin, Trotsky, Stalin* (New York, 1948) which contains some pertinent information relating to the attitudes of Marx, Lenin, and Stalin toward Poland.

There are very few works on Polish nationalism. Roman Dmowski's *Mysli Nowoczesnego Polaka* (Lwow, 1893) reveals the political philosophy of the leader of the Polish National Committee. In it the pro-Russian Dmowski advocates a racial nationalism which equals that of Hitler. The standard book on Polish nationalism is Mary M. Gardner's *Poland, A Study in National Idealism* (London, 1915). Although dated it still remains one of the best scholarly works on the subject.

There are no works which deal comprehensively with the Polish question during the first World War and its impact on the rebirth of Poland. Roman Dmowski in his interesting *La Question polonaise* (Paris, 1909) tries to arouse pro-tsarist attitudes among the

Poles. Ninian Hill's *Poland and the Polish Question* (London, 1915) is a journalistic and popular work which emphasizes the gallantry of the Poles and pleads for sympathy for Poland. Michal Bobrzynski's *Wskrzeszenie Panstwa Polskiego* (Cracow, 1920, 1925) is probably the most comprehensive treatment but is inadequate, being little more than a compilation of selective facts. The author gives more credit than is due to the Austrian Poles, while the role of America is hardly mentioned. Paul Roth's *Die Entstehung des polnischen Staates* (Berlin, 1926) presents a documentary study and interpretation of the negotiations that led to the restoration of Poland but fails to consider the American role sufficiently. For summary treatments see Szymon Askenazy's *Uwagi* (Warsaw, 1924), Stanislaw Kutrzeba's *Polska Odrodzona 1914–1928* (Cracow, 1928), and Marcelli Handselman's *Polska w Czasie Wielkiej Wojny* (Warsaw, 1932).

There are no works which deal directly with President Wilson's attitude toward Poland and the role he played in bringing about the Polish restoration in 1918. Venceslas de Tworkowski's *Wilson et la question polonaise* (Saint-Moritz, 1919) is nothing more than a polemical brochure. For an excellent background for understanding the forces shaping Wilson's attitude toward Poland see Harley Notter's *The Origins of the Foreign Policy of Woodrow Wilson* (Baltimore, 1937), Ray Stannard Baker's *Woodrow Wilson: Life and Letters* (New York, 1927–46), and Arthur S. Link's *Wilson, the Road to the White House* (Princeton, 1947).

There are many brilliant and penetrating studies of the history of immigration to America, but none of them deal directly and comprehensively with the impact of the minority groups upon American foreign policy. Carl Wittke's *We Who Build America: The Saga of the Immigrant* (New York, 1939) is a competent account of the immigrants' contributions to America but neglects to treat the influence of the immigrant groups on our foreign policy. The standard works are Marcus L. Hansen's *The Immigrant in American History* (Cambridge, Mass., 1940) and *The Atlantic Migration, 1607–1860* (Cambridge, Mass., 1940). David F. Bower's *Foreign Influences in American Life: Essays and Critical Bibliographies* (Princeton, 1944) is an excellent collection of essays, but it does not touch the problem of immigrant pressure upon American foreign policy.

The material on the Polish immigration is voluminous but of poor quality. Emily Balch's *Our Slavic Fellow Citizens* (New

York, 1910) is a general study of all the Slavic groups. William I. Thomas and Florian Znaniecki's *The Polish Peasant in Europe and America* (New York, 1927) is the best study of the Polish immigrants as a group and a classic in its field. Robert E. Park's *The Immigrant Press and Its Control* (New York, 1922) is a general study of the immigrant press. The Polish Roman Catholic Union has published many books and pamphlets. All of them lack objectivity and thorough interpretation. Some of these books are Miecislaus Haiman's *Poland and the American Revolutionary War* (Chicago, 1932), *The Fall of Poland in Contemporary American Opinion* (Chicago, 1935), *Polish Past in America, 1608–1865* (Chicago, 1939), and Arthur P. Coleman's *A New England City and the November Uprising* (Chicago, 1939). The standard works on the history of the Poles in America are Paul Fox's *The Poles in America* (New York, 1922) and H. H. Fisher's and Sidney Brooks' *America and the New Poland* (New York, 1928). Both of them are now dated. The most recent work is Karol Wachtl's *Polonja w Ameryce* (Philadelphia, 1944).

There are no works which deal exclusively with the Polish problem at the Peace Conference. The best accounts are to be found in E. M. House's and Charles Seymour's *What Really Happened at Paris: The Story of the Peace Conference, 1918–1919, by American Delegates* (New York, 1921), H. W. V. Temperley's *A History of the Peace Conference* (London, 1924), and Paul Birdsall's *Versailles Twenty Years After* (New York, 1941). A useful memoir is Stephen Bonsal's *Suitors and Suppliants: The Little Nations at Versailles* (New York, 1946). For the Polish point of view see Casimir Smogorzewski's *La Pomeranie polonaise* (Paris, 1932).

Of the many biographies and memoirs of the statesmen who played an important role during the period under discussion Roman Dmowski's *Polityka Polska i Odbudowanie Panstwa* (Warsaw, 1925) is by far the most important for understanding Polish politics. Charles Seymour's *The Intimate Papers of Colonel House* (New York, 1926–28) is full of pertinent information about the political activities of Paderewski and Dmowski in the United States. The British attitude toward Poland is expressed clearly in David Lloyd George's *Memoirs of the Peace Conference* (New Haven, 1939), while Hunter Miller's *My Diary at the Peace Conference at Paris* (1924) supplies an enormous number of documents which reveal the attitudes of the major powers toward Poland.

Other biographies and memoirs which contain useful information are Jozef Pilsudski's *Rok 1920* (Warsaw, 1924), Leon Bilinski's *Wspomnienia i Dokumenty* (Warsaw, 1925), and Rom Landau's *Ignace Paderewski, Musician and Statesman* (New York, 1936). The latter suffers from a pro-Paderewski bias. The chapters on the political activities of Paderewski are general. Some of the data used were found to be erroneous.

The most valuable private papers are those of Col. E. M. House. His voluminous diary and correspondence contain material of great historical importance. The same thing is true of the excellent collection of Woodrow Wilson's papers. Each complements the other. The Frank Polk and William Wiseman papers, which are a part of the House Collection, are important addenda to the above two.

Appendix

The following is the editorial in English from *Zgoda*, Chicago, February 21, 1920:

The Polish Daily *Zgoda* henceforth will devote some of its columns to news items and editorials in the English language.

The first of these editorials will appear in Tuesday's issue.

We reach the Polish-speaking people throughout this land. Our editorials and news items are read with interest by the big masses of the Polish-speaking people in this country and across the Atlantic. The Polish press, here and abroad, quotes our opinion frequently.

We say this in no other sense than as a statement of fact, that our voice reaches large masses of people spread over a vast territory.

This newspaper is an American institution. We preached Americanism —true, loyal, and unwavering Americanism, not only during and after the war, but before the war. It was in the past, and is to-day, our policy to keep the Polish-speaking people in continuous contact with America and American institutions. We have endeavored at all times to lead along the path to a big, powerful, and prosperous America; to a united, law-abiding, contented, and happy nation.

We continue this work and in this leadership.

And, as we continue, our work increases and our task grows bigger. It is not sufficient to make America, and all that concerns America, understood to the people whom we lead. We must also make these people, their traditions, their past, and their present, understood by America. Nothing short of mutual understanding can bring about the results hoped for by all lovers of America and Americanism.

Therein lies the reason for our decision to run some of our columns in the English language. . . .

We will present in these English columns to those who understand neither the Polish language nor the Polish people, the case of those millions of men and women of Polish blood who aided not only willingly and faithfully, but lovingly, in making the United States the greatest country in the world; who through their labors and sacrifices added materially to the wealth and strength of this country.

There are a number of matters, vital to this country, that these people —our people and your people—wish to present in the public forum. It is our duty to act for them.

We will carry their voice beyond the confines of their own ranks. . . .

Our columns in English will be edited by John A. Wedda, an American newspaper man of many years' experience.

The following is the editorial in Polish from the same newspaper of the same date:

In our issue of February 24th, of the *Zgoda,* will appear the first editorial printed in the English language, and from now on we will regularly insert articles in English on subjects interesting to us. In to-day's English article we explain to our readers, and also to Anglo-Americans, why the *Zgoda,* being an exclusively Polish newspaper, will henceforth devote some space to articles in English, which space will be enlarged in the future accordingly.

We stipulate, saying this openly because publicly, that we are not doing this out of any Americanization motive, for we resent forcible and silly efforts in that direction. Our aim in doing this is to provide means of self-defense to Polish emigration, so their voice would be heard in things most vital to them, and reach where it should.

America is beginning to ail with chauvinism, which is most detrimental to the nation and country.

As a result of this some Senators and Representatives have already gone mad and are submitting bills to Congress which the most violent "Hakatist" representatives in the German parliament would not dare to do. To this action, which tends to destroy the Polish spirit in the United States, we must answer with self-defense.

According to the decision of Zarazd Centralny Z.N.P. (Central Committee of Polish National Alliance), the informational article will be edited by Mr. J. Wedda.

But this has a wider scope: the flow of Polish emigration from Europe in the future will cease almost entirely; therefore, the Polish National Alliance will be to develop on the American soil only, among the youth born and brought up in America, the American Poles. So it is desirable that they early become acquainted with the object of the Alliance through these informational articles, also become used to the *Zgoda,* and slowly become acquainted with its Polish contents. It is a very serious undertaking which interests us all; to "Polonize" is the reason why the English section in the *Zgoda* is coming to life.

As further evidence of the necessity of this, is an article which ought to stir the minds of all American Poles, which we are printing to-day under the heading "Polish Catholic Blood on Sale." The voice of our indignation and protest should reach the highest places, but no matter how we raise our voices it will be of no use if it is in Polish. If we want results, as citizens of this country we must come out in a language which is understood by everyone who has been in America for some time—the language of the American people.

For these and many other reasons, on the eve of the one hundred and eighty-eighth anniversary of the great Washington—the creator and father of this country, which, according to his ideals, was to shine forever with unrestrained freedom and citizenship, tolerance, language, and belief—we are forced into a position of self-defense by those who through the example of Washington ought to be fathers and not step-fathers to all seeking the protection of the Star Spangled Banner. May this become our shield and be of benefit to our adopted country.

Cited in Robert E. Park, *The Immigrant Press and Its Control* (New York and London, Harper, 1922), pp. 210–13.

The Preliminary Confidential Memorandum by John Dewey to Colonel House on the Detroit Convention

Courtesy House Collection, Yale University Library

August 19, 1918.

PRELIMINARY CONFIDENTIAL MEMORANDUM
Re Detroit Convention.

PENDING the preparation of a more extensive report, as asked for by the Military Intelligence Branch, I beg leave to submit a preliminary report concerning activities in connection with the Detroit Convention. This Convention is convened for August 26th, and accordingly presents the only immediate and urgent phase of the matter.

I. Character of Convention.

The Convention is called by a committee having headquarters in Chicago, calling itself A National Department. This central committee appointed a pre-convention committee, consisting in part of its own members and in part of other individuals affiliated with them, which issued rules concerning both the appointment of delegates and the actual conduct of the convention when called. It will be noted them that the conduct of the convention is not under its own control. The convention is ostensibly called to express authoritatively the "external will" of the entire Polish immigration regarding the Polish press, including a large number which have supported the National Department in the past and societies affiliated with it, shows a great deal of friction and discontent. The vagueness and complexity of the rules regarding the appointment of delegates, the assumption of authority on the part of the National Department to decide whether a given organization comes within the list of those who are entitled to send delegates, appear to justify the suspicions and criticism that the convention is not in fact what it purports to be. The rules for conducting the convention place the actual business of the convention in thousands of six sections, the President, Secretary, and nine members of which are to be appointed by the Chairman of the Convention; more-over, the pre-Convention committee appoints in advance clerks who draw up a list of topics to be considered by these sections. Only at the last day of the convention does the convention as a whole take action beyound listening to speeches and reports, any discussion of which is officially discouraged. On the last day the entire convention can take action only upon resolutions reported to it from the section. There can be no discussion of these section reports excepting upon the written request of one-third of the members of the convention.

These facts explain the very general criticism and unfavorable comment of a very considerable portion of the Polish press. Unless very great care is taken in the actual conduct of the convention to allay suspicion and mistrust by a frank and open policy they render it practically impossible for the convention to speak with that authority and unity which are most desirable. It should be clear that the criticisms to which reference is made are in no sense confined to the K.O.N., or radical faction.

II. The Convention and Polish Finances.

There is an immense dis-satisfaction among practically all groups of Poles with the management of their financial affairs. There are constant recrimmination and counter-charges, leaving entirely out of account the accusation of misuse of funds; these charges concern extravagant salaries, unnecessary duplication of societies and offices, and failure to discriminate between funds raised for distinctly relief purposes, for propaganda and press-work, for political and for army purposes. There is jealousy at least between the Chicago headquarters, which handles funds, and the large number of the local organizations that raise the funds. Since the parish priests who are in closest contact with the mass of Polish population are largely instrumental in the raising of local funds the charges and counter-charges are having a decidedly bad effect upon the mass of Polish immigrants. It is reported,—and so far as we can determine, correctly,—that funds collected last May are still witheld from transmission to headquarters. All Poles are much dis-satisfied with the relatively small amount of money that has been raised for Polish purposes in this country. Attempts to explain this small fund have led Poles now very influential in the conduct of their affairs in this country to attact Americans for lack of interest, to attack the conduct of the Red Cross, and to the recriminations among themselves to which attention has already been called.

The situation has lately been further complicated by the introduction of the so-called "White Cross", Although in France the corresponding society for the relief of Polish soldiers works under the French Red Cross, the so-called "White Cross in this country is working independently. The masses of the Polish people do not understand why they should not work with the under the American Red Cross, and the attempt of the authorities of the White Cross to answer questions and criticisms leads to attacks on the American Red Cross. In addition, the duplication of offices and salaries is criticised. It is a part of the task of the Convention to straighten out these various matters, secure unity and eficiency, of raising and distributing funds. According to all information at our hand this can really be accomplished only in one way,—namely, unification under representative Americans who have the confidence both of Polish immigrants and of generous Americans. Anything short of this will be regarded by very numerous sections of the Polish immigrants as merely an attempt to perpetuate with minor changes the confusion and rivalry which has so unfortunately existed in the past. The interest of the American Government and policy in this matter is obvious. The present situation re-acts unfavorably upon the recruiting and support of the Polish Army, of the American Red Cross—of which the President of the United States is President—, and tends to create totally unnecessary divisions and quarrels of the Polish civilian population, which is enthusiastically united otherwise in support of the war. Moreover, the comparatively small amount of funds raised for Polish affairs as compared with that for other oppressed nationalities of Europe re-acts unfavorably upon American prestige abroad.

All factions of the Poles are so committed to the expressed policies of President Wilson about the war in general, and the future of Poland in particular, that it would be an easy matter for a few words from the right sources to bring about the required unity and efficiency under definitely American auspices. Obviously any hesitation in acceding to such a request would indicate that personal or factional ambition is more influential than loyalty to the United States or even to Poland.

III. Political Aspects of the Convention.

Some weeks ago a bill was prepared to be introduced in the Senate of the United States, one of the provisions of which was a clause which virtually constituted a committee located in Paris as the State and War Department of the new united and independent Poland. It is reported that this bill was prepared or transmitted through the agency of the Polish press bureau of Washington. Our information is to the effect that the actual introduction of this bill was delayed at the suggestion of high governmental authorities. Our information is also to the effect that an important representative of one of the foreign military commissions in this country stated that the General Staffs of both France and Great Britain were desirous of securing such recognition of the Paris Committee, but that the American Government up to this time had blocked such action. We have Mr. Paderewski's personal statement that attempts to make the Paris Committee more representative by including members of the parties of the Left, and a very influential representative of the Austrian socialists, (who while on Austrian soil had come out strongly for a free and united Poland with access to the sea), had been over-ruled by representatives of the military staff of Great Britain and France,—a fact which would presumptively indicate an interest of the American War Department in this whole situation.

In view of the fact that the persons in control of the convention had prepared a resolution which purports to voice the will of the entire Polish immigration in this country in favor of making the Paris Committee the Foreign and War Department of the New State of Poland, it is a fair inference that one of the main objects of the convention was to bring pressure to bear upon the American Government. If this had been done at the request of the President through the State and War Department there is of course, nothing further to be said; but if the resolution was prepared without a frank and complete understanding with the State and War Department the resolution appears to indicate a willingness to subordinate American to foreign interests.

In this connection it is appropriate to call attention to two facts; One is that President Wilson and the American Government are the only authorities which have the complete confidence of all Poles in this country and abroad. President Wilson, in his speech of January 22, 1917, was the first statesman to go out for a free and united Poland. Moreover, owing to past historic complication the United States is the only country which is trusted by the Poles here and abroad as completely dis-interested in its policy in the peace settlement as that affects Poland. Under such circumstances American leadership is as natural as pressure from a convention misrepresenting itself as the voice of all Poles in behalf of foreign leadership would be distressing and unfortunate. The other fact is that Mr. Paderewski is the official delegate of the Paris Committee to this country; that he speaks of himself as a "plenipotentiary", and is freely spoken of by his immediate associates as Ambassador of Poland to the United States.

IV. Summary.

It is in the interest of complete Polish unity in this country and of American influence and prestige abroad, both in general and with reference to Poland in particular, that the Detroit Convention be postponed until there is adequate assurance that it is genuinely representative in its make-up and truly parliamentary in its procedure, and is committed to a policy which has the antecedent sanction of the State and War Department of the United States.

If such postponement is now impossible, then it is important that the convention, through the comparatively small group in control of it, be guided in the direction indicated above. Namely, first, financial reorganization and unification, with sufficient active, not merely nominal, American representation to secure confidence and supervise methods and details of collection, distribution and accounting, together with added Polish members drawn from persons not identified with any of the present contending interests; there are a number of those who have withdrawn because of disgust at squabbles and personal intrigue. Second, with reference to foreign affairs a resolution calling for an American commission which shall have as its object the unification of all Polish groups and parties in behalf of the declared policies of President Wilson, and which shall—through authorized representatives—get in touch with similar groups abroad, including those in Poland itself. We are assured by representatives in high standing of both the more conservative and the more radical party groups in this country, that in spite of German occupation such communication is entirely feasible, and in fact is now maintained.

The willingness to accede to such a proposition would be an acid test of whether the interests of the United States primarily, and of Poland secondarily, are uppermost, or whether these interests are subordinate to something personal and factional. This test should be applied to the representatives of all groups whatsoever, and they should be judged by results.

If there are wieghty and important objections to the course outlined it certainly would be a simple matter to pass a resolution stating that the Poles of this country unitedly and enthusiastically in the future interests of their country to the leadership of President Wilson. If instead of such a resolution any individual prefers a resolution in behalf of any committee on foreign shores, no matter how influential in the past it would seem to fix his status beyond further discussion.

August 20, 1918.

Later information shows that one faction plans to eliminate Madame Paderewski from financial and internal activity. If she declines, it will be put up to Mr. Paderewski. If he refuses, he will be told that he also must withdraw from connection with financial and American Polish affairs; that he is to be "promoted" to Washington to take care of the international end, in view of the fact that he is a delegate from the Paris Committee.

The significant bearing of this is in connection with the proposed resolution recommending making the Paris Committee the State and War Departments of the new State of Poland. The larger number of the Poles are not particularly interested in the international complications, or are ignorant of them this element would have favored the passing of the resolution simply as a method of eliminating the Paderewski influence in domestic and financial affairs to this country. This comes in part from the section which is honestly disgusted with the Paderewski regime, and in part from those who wish to have the management of funds in their own hands, in this country.

All of this strife is, of course, within parties nominally supporting the present Paderewski and Chicago Groups.

Respectfully submitted,

JOHN DEWEY.

amh.

SECOND PRELIMINARY MEMORANDUM—
CONFIDENTIAL POLISH CONDITIONS
IN THIS COUNTRY

Publicity.

Aug. 23, 1918

The question of publicity for Poland and Polish affairs is urgent.

1. There is immense dissatisfaction among the Poles with the *amount* of publicity given to the Polish cause. Poland is both the largest and the most important from all points of view of the oppressed nationalities of Europe for whose freedom we are fighting. Poles point out that it will rank, even immediately after the war, next to Spain, or form the seventh country in population in Europe; that its geographical position makes it the key to the future war and peace relations of eastern and even south-eastern Europe; that its political problems are more complicated than those of any other oppressed nationality, owing to its past division between three great powers, and of the peculiar importance of the relations of Poland to the Jews, Lithuanians, and Ruthenians. In addition they point to the antecedent sentimental interest of Americans in Poland, which would have been intensified by an adequate knowledge of the sufferings of Poland as great as those of Belgium or Serbia. The domestic American interest is pointed to in connection with the fact that the Poles are about one-twentieth of our population, one sixth or seventh of our total immigration population, and that the Labor and Immigration problems after the war, as well as those of establishing the best commercial relations with the new State of Poland, make wide publicity most important.

After reciting such facts as these, they point to the great ignorance among even educated Americans of Polish questions, and to the fact that there is next to no publicity. They compare the amount of space given to Polish affairs to that, say, of the Checko-Slovaks, and show that what does find its way into the American press almost comes thru regular foreign press channels, and that no attempt is made to show the meaning or bearing of this material from week to week and day to day.

2. The blame for this state of affairs is put upon the Polish Press Bureau or socalled Polish Associated Press located in Washington. Charges of both ignorance, inefficiency, and lack of vigor are freely made. It is said that Mr. White's past record does not justify his being head of the Bureau, that he owes his position there to Mr. Paderewski's influence and financial support rather than general ability or special knowledge of Polish affairs; that Mr. Wedda, an American Pole, is not expert in the Polish language and that he owes his position to his former connection with Mr. Smulski. As there is reported friction between the Paderewski group and the Chicago group headed by Smulski (in spite of external show of har-

mony), it is said that they are there to see that both factions receive attention. There is said to be a Pole connected with the Bureau who is much
better informed about Polish affairs and abler, but who is very lazy—
unfortunately I have mislaid the memorandum of his name. In connection
with the charge of lack of energy brought against the whole Bureau, it is
pointed out that of the issues of Free Poland, a monthly in the English
language for publicity among Americans, the June number did not come
out till well in August; the charge of ignorance is specifically supported
by the instance of the appeal for funds in that issue for support of the
Polish army in which the simple facts about the army were misstated and
had the effect of discouraging recruiting as well as casting reflections upon
the French management of its affairs, on account of gross understatement
of pay, privileges, etc.

3. In addition to claims of ignorance and inefficiency as accounting for
the lack of adequate publicity, it is said that the Bureau is much more concerned with furthering the fortunes of a faction of Poles in this country
than of presenting the interests of the Polish cause; that it has permitted
itself to become the headquarters of intrigue, malicious gossip, and other
activities calculated to divide the Poles. I have in my possession a memorandum coming from quarters directly connected with the Polish Press Bureau supporting this charge. The factional tendencies among Poles are
already so strong that it is impossible to overstate the dangerous and un-
American character of all activities that tend to further dissension and
discord.

4. As also accounting for the absence of genuine publicity thru this
Bureau, the close personal relations mentioned above, between its members
and Messrs. Paderewski and Smulski are pointed to. It is generally believed—this among Poles of almost every faction—that the Bureau has
concerned itself more with personal press agency work for Mme and
Mr. Paderewski than with systematic and whole-hearted general Polish
propaganda. This general belief is doing so much harm that it should be
looked into, so that the situation may be radically changed if the charge
is true, and authoritatively put to rest if it is at fault. The inquiry should
not rest with personal assertions pro or con but include examination of
financial support and expenditures.

5. The Government has a double interest in this situation, in addition
to the general interest in adequate publicity, and in addition to the bearing of this publisity upon the matters already pointed out, namely, (a)
better relations between Poles in America and other Americans, (b) dis-
couragement of factions and securing of unity, (c) recruiting for the
Polish army from Class Five. These are—

I. The War Department now refers all press inquirers and others to
the Bureau for all information regarding the Polish army. This tends
practically, if not officially, to give it a semi-official status for Washington
reporters as sources for all Polish affairs.

II. Mr. Wedda is the Chairman of the section of the C.P I for Polish affairs, and his office in such capacity is adjacent to his office in his capacity as member of the Polish Press Bureau.

Recommendations

1. An official inquiry into the efficiency, intelligence and affiliations of the Bureau. This should, as stated above, go into matters of finance as well as effect some showdown as to what the Bureau has been accomplishing.

2. An immediate termination of Mr. Wedda's connection with the C P I.

3. The development of a well-considered and effective organization for Polish publicity whose main objects should be:

1. Securing and publishing full information about all phases of the Polish problem general knowledge of which among Americans and the Polish Immigration would unify and intensify support of the war.

2. Bringing about greater unity among the Poles, reducing and eliminating so far as possible their cut throat and factional metjods.

Senator JOHN W. KERN of *Indiana:*—"The Polish-Americans in South Bend and other parts of northern Indiana cast a large Democratic vote. In fact, I think our success in St. Joseph county, in which the city of South Bend is situated, was due largely to the Polish-American vote."

Senator GILBERT M. HITCHCOCK of *Nebraska:*—"The proportion of Poles voting for the President was very large,—in fact, I should say from my observation in Nebraska that it was overwhelming, say 85 percent."

Senator ATLEE POMERENE of *Ohio:*—"An overwhelming majority of the Polish voters in Cleveland were for President Wilson. There is a large Polish vote in Toledo and a relatively large Polish vote in a number of other Ohio cities. What is true of the Polish vote in Cleveland is true in the other Ohio cities as well."

Former Congressman ROBERT J. BULKLEY of *Ohio,* Director of the Naturalized Citizens' Bureau at the Western Headquarters of the Democratic National Committee:—"There is no doubt that the Poles in Cleveland voted overwhelmingly for the President. In other Ohio cities the result was about the same as in Cleveland."

Congressman HENRY A. BARNHART of *Indiana:*—"In South Bend, the large Polish vote was almost solid for President Wilson and the same I think was true in Michigan City."

Congressman CARL C. VAN DYKE of *Minnesota:*—"We carried every Polish locality for Wilson."

Congressman JOHN A. M. ADAIR, of *Indiana,* also candidate for Governor:—"At least 75 per cent of the Polish vote went to the President.

In northern Indiana, especially in St. Joseph County, the Polish vote was very largely for President Wilson."

Congressman ISAAC R. SHERWOOD of *Ohio:*—"At least ninety per cent of the vote in Toledo, Ohio, was cast for President Wilson. The majority for President Wilson in the Polish district was overwhelming."

Congressman THOMAS F. KONOP of *Wisconsin:*—"I believe 75 per cent of the citizens of Polish origin voted for Hon. Woodrow Wilson for President. I do not believe I am exaggerating when I make that statement. The Polish precincts in my District gave substantial majorities for Wilson."

Congressman D. J. RIORDAN of *New York:*—"The Polish people here in my State voted as a unit for President Wilson and the whole Democratic ticket."

IGNATIUS K. WERWINSKI, Democratic leader of *Indiana:*—"In South Bend, in three Polish wards, Wilson obtained a plurality of 1289. Most of our people voted for Wilson. In the cities of La Porte, New Carlisle, Valparaiso, Mishawaka, Michigan City, Fort Wayne, Terre Haute, Indianapolis, Hammond, Whiting, East Chicago, Indiana Harbor and Aetna the Polish people gave a large plurality to Wilson."

Congressman MICHAEL F. PHELAN of *Massachusetts:*—"In my section most of the Polish vote went Democratic."

Congressman JAMES A. HAMILL of *New Jersey:*—"I have been informed on very reliable authority that a majority of the Polish people in New Jersey voted for President Wilson."

STATE OF MISSOURI

Population of Polish origin approximates 300,000.
Estimated Polish vote—about 90 per cent Democratic.
President Wilson's plurality—28,659.

STATE OF NEBRASKA

Population of Polish descent—over 125,000.
The Polish vote, according to Senator Hitchcock, was 85 per cent Democratic.
President Wilson's plurality—41,056.

STATE OF NORTH DAKOTA

Several large and small settlements of Polish farmers.
Overwhelming majority for President Wilson in Polish precincts.
President Wilson's plurality—1,735.

STATE OF OHIO

Urban and rural population of Polish origin—nearly half a million.
Proportion voting for President Wilson estimated as high as 90 per cent.
President Wilson's plurality—90,408.

Estimates and Ex-parte Fragmentary Tabulation of the Polish-American Vote in the 1916 Election, Submitted by the Democratic National Committee for Colonel House

Courtesy House Collection, Yale University Library

1916 NOVEMBER ELECTION

Banner Ward of ALL Chicago

WARD 16 PRECINCT			Wilson		Hughes	
			Men	Women	Men	Women
Polish		1	135	79	59	16
"		2	165	61	55	14
"		3	146	67	35	11
"	& Irish	4	125	58	66	23
"		5	157	72	54	32
"	& German	6	145	61	96	33
"		7	143	62	56	32
"	& German	8	74	65	72	36
"	& Irish	9	147	56	65	17
"	"	10	148	63	53	6
"		11	140	57	34	17
"		12	165	61	12	19
"		13	181	77	34	10
"		14	138	39	46	12
"		15	152	105	44	16
"		16	167	85	31	17
"		17	106	98	34	15
"		18	184	100	45	16
"		19	130	56	44	21
"		20	169	114	55	16
"		21	159	74	49	15
"		22	88	59	15	14
"		23	202	84	27	9
"		24	172	115	25	9
"	& German	25	136	65	73	29
"	"	26	138	56	80	25
"	& Jewish	27	115	47	94	41
Jewish & Polish		28	120	87	89	60
Polish		29	167	66	63	22
"	& Jewish	30	131	98	46	19
Jewish & Polish		31	88	29	34	4
"	"	32	78	51	50	24
"		33	82	44	65	23
		34	4,592	2,311	1,700	673
		35				
		36				
		37				
		38				

Per Cent Distribution of the Popular Vote
for President, by Parties

Courtesy of the Republican National Headquarters

	1912				1916	
	Per cent Dem.	Per cent Rep.	Per cent Prog.	Per cent Rep. & Prog.	Per cent Dem.	Per cent Rep.
NEW ENGLAND						
Maine	39.4	20.5	37.4	57.9	47.0	51.0
New Hampshire	39.5	37.4	20.2	57.6	49.1	49.05
Vermont	24.4	37.1	35.2	72.3	35.2	62.4
Massachusetts	35.6	31.9	29.1	61.0	46.6	50.5
Rhode Island	39.0	35.6	21.7	57.3	46.0	51.1
Connecticut	39.2	35.9	17.9	53.8	46.7	49.8
Total	36.7	32.3	27.1	59.4	46.2	51.1
MIDDLE ATLANTIC						
New York	41.3	28.7	24.6	53.3	44.5	50.9
New Jersey	41.2	20.5	33.6	54.1	42.7	54.4
Pennsylvania	32.5	22.4	36.5	58.9	40.2	54.3
Total	38.0	25.2	30.3	55.5	42.7	52.7
EAST NORTH CENTRAL						
Ohio	41.0	26.8	22.2	49.0	51.9	44.1
Indiana	43.1	23.1	24.8	47.9	46.5	47.4
Illinois	35.3	22.1	33.7	55.8	43.4	52.6
Michigan	27.4	27.6	38.9	66.5	43.9	52.2
Wisconsin	41.1	32.7	15.6	48.3	42.8	49.4
Total	37.7	25.5	27.8	53.3	45.8	49.7
WEST NORTH CENTRAL						
Minnesota	31.8	19.2	37.7	56.9	46.25	46.34
Iowa	37.6	24.3	32.9	57.2	42.9	54.3
Missouri	47.3	29.7	17.8	47.5	50.6	46.9
North Dakota	34.2	26.5	29.8	56.3	47.8	46.3
South Dakota	41.8	——	50.2	50.2	45.9	49.8
Nebraska	43.7	21.7	29.1	50.8	55.3	41.0
Kansas	39.3	20.5	32.9	53.4	50.0	44.0
Total	40.7	23.2	29.4	52.6	48.6	47.0
SOUTH ATLANTIC						
Delaware	46.5	32.9	18.2	51.1	47.8	50.2
Maryland	48.6	23.7	24.9	48.6	52.8	44.8
Virginia	—	—	—	—	—	—
West Virginia	42.8	21.5	29.9	51.4	48.4	49.4
North Carolina	—	—	—	—	—	—
South Carolina	—	—	—	—	—	—
Georgia	—	—	—	—	—	—
Florida	—	—	—	—	—	—
Total	57.6	16.6	22.9	39.5	60.7	35.8

Per Cent Distribution of the Popular Vote
for President, by Parties

	1912				1916	
	Per cent Dem.	Per cent Rep.	Per cent Prog.	Per cent Rep. & Prog.	Per cent Dem.	Per cent Rep.
EAST SOUTH CENTRAL						
Kentucky	48.5	25.5	22.5	48.0	51.9	46.5
Tennessee	52.6	23.9	21.7	45.6	56.2	42.8
Alabama	——	——	——	——	——	——
Mississippi	——	——	——	——	——	——
Total	55.4	21.1	20.6	41.7	59.7	38.8
WEST SOUTH CENTRAL						
Arkansas	——	——	——	——	——	——
Louisiana	——	——	——	——	——	——
Oklahoma	47.1	35.7	——	35.7	50.6	33.3
Texas	——	——	——	——	——	——
Total	61.8	19.4	7.6	27.0	67.7	23.3
MOUNTAIN						
Montana	35.0	23.2	28.1	51.3	56.9	37.6
Idaho	32.1	31.1	24.1	55.2	52.0	41.1
Wyoming	36.2	34.4	21.8	56.2	54.6	41.9
Colorado	42.9	21.9	27.0	48.9	60.7	34.8
New Mexico	41.4	35.9	16.9	52.8	50.3	46.5
Arizona	51.0	14.7	34.3	49.0	57.2	35.4
Utah	32.6	37.5	21.5	59.0	58.8	37.8
Nevada	39.7	15.9	27.9	43.8	53.4	36.4
Total	38.3	27.3	25.0	52.3	57.0	37.9
PACIFIC						
Washington	27.0	21.9	35.3	57.2	48.1	43.9
Oregon	34.3	25.3	27.4	52.7	45.9	48.5
California	41.8	0.6	41.8	42.4	46.6	46.3
Total	36.7	9.6	38.3	47.9	46.9	46.1
GRAND TOTAL	41.9	23.2	27.4	50.6	49.3	46.1

Index